MEXICO
IN YOUR KITCHEN

Favorite Mexican Recipes That Celebrate
Family, Community, Culture, and Tradition

Mely Martínez

ROCK
POINT

First published in 2024 by Rock Point, an imprint of The Quarto Group,
142 West 36th Street, 4th Floor, New York, NY 10018, USA
(212) 779-4972 www.Quarto.com

Rock Point titles are also available at discount for retail, wholesale, promotional and bulk purchase. For details, contact the Special Sales Manager by email at specialsales@quarto.com or by mail at The Quarto Group, Attn: Special Sales Manager, 100 Cummings Center Suite, 265D, Beverly, MA 01915, USA.

10 9 8 7 6 5 4 3 2 1

ISBN: 978-1-63106-937-6

Digital edition published in 2024
eISBN: 978-0-7603-8130-4

Library of Congress Control Number: 2023948739

Publisher: Rage Kindelsperger
Creative Director: Laura Drew
Editorial Director: Erin Canning
Managing Editor: Cara Donaldson
Cover and Interior Design: Laura Klynstra
Photography: David Castañeda and Adriana Byers
Author Photos (pages 6 and 240): Terri Glanger

Printed in China

To David A.

CONTENTS

DRINKS

SIDES, SALSAS & PEPPERS

DESSERTS & BREADS

INTRODUCTION

This book builds upon the warm reception of my previous one, *The Mexican Home Kitchen*. That book features many basic recipes that are easy to understand for newcomers to Mexican home cooking. It was envisioned as a way to introduce them to the fundamentals of Mexican cuisine and teach how to prepare foods such as tortillas, salsas, rice, beans, and the most commonly known stews and dishes. I do reference a lot of those recipes throughout this book and have included a handy guide in the back to remind you of the recipes found in *The Mexican Home Kitchen*.

This book delves further into the Mexican gastronomy, featuring recipes from all corners of the country. You will learn how to make the sides, soups, stews, and even breakfasts that are enjoyed every day by people all over Mexico, including dishes that are not often found on restaurant menus and remain cherished family recipes that are prepared exclusively at home. I have included a section on Mexican food customs so that you can get to know how and when these dishes are consumed during an average day in Mexico, as well as how important it is for Mexicans to use food as a time to gather with loved ones.

Moving outside of the Mexican home kitchen, I have included a brand-new section on *antojitos*. These are the foods that are commonly found at street stands in Mexican cities and are the savory treats that are made with masa dough, such as sopes, gorditas, and, of course, corn tortilla tacos. Additionally, this book will introduce you to the world of Mexican baking. While Mexicans love bread (both savory and sweet), few make it at home. It is more common to buy bread at neighborhood bakeries, called *panaderias*. Some of the panaderia classics you will find here include conchas, bollilos, and mantecadas.

Selecting the recipes for this book was no small task, considering the vastness of Mexican cuisine and the many beloved dishes that are part of it. I wanted to choose recipes that people will truly enjoy and want to make for their families again and again. Every recipe I have chosen is one that I have made in my own home many times, so you can be sure they are tried and tested. All you have to do is choose which ones are your favorites!

The dishes in this book vary in scale and complexity. Some can be made every day, while a few of them are more common for weekends or special gatherings. Additionally, some dishes are well known in a particular part of the country but may sound strange to people who don't live in that region, so don't be afraid to try something new, even if a recipe sounds intimidating or unfamiliar. Rest assured, regardless of where they are from, each dish in this book is beloved by many families who eat it regularly, and a lot of these recipes are surprisingly easy to make. A few examples are olla tapada and pollo a las finas Hierbas, which not everyone in Mexico is aware of but are delicious and simple to prepare.

As with my first book, I've taken a great deal of time ensuring that every recipe has valuable and informative notes to help you prepare these dishes with confidence. Before you start cooking, I highly recommend that you thoroughly study each recipe, its ingredients, and the notes (Notas). These notes will tell you what to serve with each dish, as well as how to make substitutions (if needed), store the leftovers (if any), and source specific ingredients. You will find a lot of tips in there, and sometimes even a bonus recipe within the recipe!

Whether it be a homestyle breakfast dish, an elegant Sunday-dinner stew, or street-style tacos, the recipes contained in this book will help you further explore the world of Mexican cuisine and all it has to offer. You will be able to eat as if you spent an entire day in Mexico, from breakfast to dinner to dessert. My hope is that the recipes in this book will become cherished favorites in your kitchen, enjoyed by your family time and time again, just as they are in mine.

Embrace the tradition of sobremesa—spending quality time together after a meal—creating lasting memories and stronger bonds with your loved ones through the joy of food.

Buen provecho!

MEXICAN FOOD CUSTOMS

Food is an incredibly essential part of daily life in Mexico, and it is often intertwined with our social life too. Breakfast and lunch are important times spent with family, and dinner is an excellent way to socialize with friends and colleagues.

The best meals are the ones with plenty of *sobremesa*, which is the word for the time spent after the meal, when everyone stays at the table to continue chatting. Lengthy chats can even be had over a cup of coffee and some bread or cookies. For Mexicans, food and drink are often the best way to create quality time with loved ones.

Like in a lot of countries, there are many dishes that are only eaten for certain meals of the day. Some foods are even reserved for weekends only. Below, I give a brief explanation of each meal of the day and what foods are commonly prepared for them.

DESAYUNO

Desayuno, or breakfast, can take many forms depending on one's lifestyle and the region they live in. When it comes to simple breakfasts, a lot of people will have a cup of coffee alongside a piece of toast or *pan dulce* (sweet bread). When my siblings and I were growing up, breakfast usually consisted of a glass of coffee with milk and a piece of toasted Bolillo (page 215) with butter on it. In rural Mexico, some farm workers will have a cup of thick *atole*. These light meals are more common with people who are early risers.

A Mexican breakfast can also be hearty and more substantial. Many breakfast meals are centered around an egg dish such as Huevos en Salsa (page 28), Huevos Rancheros (page 24), or Huevos con Chorizo (page 27). These will often be accompanied by a side of beans, a salsa, tortillas (or bread), and some fresh fruit or juice.

The home kitchen isn't the only place where you can find breakfast in Mexico, as there is a whole world of breakfast street food to enjoy. The street food can vary greatly with the region, but you will often find breakfast tacos and Gorditas (page 53). In some places, like in the center of the country, a lot of street vendors sell tamales and hot atole from their carts. You can also find juice stands that sell freshly prepared fruit juices and smoothies. All these breakfast street stands commonly serve students, office workers, and people who work in town.

ALMUERZO AND WEEKEND ALMUERZO

The term *almuerzo* can have different meanings among Spanish-speaking countries, but in Mexico, it is used to refer to a meal taken during the late morning (around 9 to 11 a.m.). It is a heavier meal than desayuno and is often eaten by people who had a light breakfast (such as coffee and bread), or who skipped breakfast entirely. An almuerzo will generally include hearty dishes such as Huevos con Chorizo (page 27), Salchichas a la Mexicana (page 47), and Chilaquiles (page 34).

Weekend almuerzo is a heavier meal that can be compared to brunch in other countries. A lot of people don't have almuerzo during the week, and the weekend is the only time when they can get together and have a late breakfast with their families. Some Mexican families will gather two or three generations at home or a restaurant to enjoy a bountiful spread of Mexican dishes.

All the breakfast dishes eaten throughout the week can be enjoyed for weekend almuerzo, but in addition to those, dishes such as barbacoa, tamales, Cochinita Pibil (page 113), menudo, Sopes (page 55), enchiladas, and more are also served. The dishes that are specially prepared for the weekends (such as menudo and barbacoa) can also vary with the region.

LUNCH

In Mexico, the main meal of the day is *comida*, or lunch, which usually takes place between 1 and 3 p.m. Most schoolchildren have already returned home by this time, and in many places, office workers are allowed to go home for their lunch breaks to eat with their families. Tradespeople will also pause their work to do the same. This practice of going home to eat lunch is slowly becoming less common, as the work schedules of some companies and the distances in the larger cities make it difficult.

A common Mexican lunch will consist of a stew served with one or two sides. The most common sides are rice and beans, although certain dishes are accompanied by mashed potatoes, spaghetti, or other side dishes. Warm tortillas and a salsa will also be on the table. For a more complete lunch spread, the main dish can also be preceded by a salad and a small serving of soup, like sopa de fideo. To drink, most Mexicans will have an agua fresca, a lemonade, or a soft drink.

The people who do not go home for lunch will often pack a lunch, but there are also many places where they can get food around town. The street food stands in the city often sell tortas (sandwiches), and there are small eateries called *fondas* that serve more homestyle meals consisting of stews and sides. In addition to fondas, there are smaller eateries called *cocinas economicas* that also sell homestyle dishes, but are primarily focused on to-go orders, and will sometimes have a more limited menu with a special of the day.

MERIENDA

Merienda is a light meal eaten during the late afternoon, around 5 or 6 p.m. It can take many forms, such as a fruit salad, a small sandwich, a tamal, some milk and cookies, a cup of atole, or a cup of coffee with pan dulce. A lot of people who take merienda have it as their last meal of the day and don't have dinner.

In Mexico, having bread with coffee during the late afternoon or early evening is the most common type of merienda. Some people will not even refer to it as *merienda,* and, instead, call it *la hora del café* (coffee time), or *el cafecito*.

CENA

Mexicans usually have *cena*, or dinner, later, generally after 7 p.m., with some people having it as late as 9 or 10 p.m. A common dinner at home can be light and consist of a small sandwich, a quesadilla, or even bread and milk (similar to a merienda). Some people will even prepare a light meal by making a breakfast dish, such as Molletes (page 40) or Migas (page 36).

When it comes to *antojitos* (street food), dinner is when the street-stand scene really comes to life. Tacos and other antojitos are primarily offered for dinner, and there are many taco stands that don't open until the evening. A lot of the stands and restaurants that sell tacos and antojitos are only open from Friday to Sunday, which is when most people like going out for dinner with friends or family.

THE MEXICAN PANTRY

Part of what makes the Mexican gastronomy so rich and interesting is its large variety of regional and seasonal dishes. No two regions of Mexico are the same, and as you travel through the country, there will always be new dishes, ingredients, and food customs to discover. Despite all this diversity, one thing that I find so beautiful about Mexican cuisine is how our cooking is very often centered around a proven collection of classic ingredients that define our national cuisine. At the center of it all is corn masa, which can take the form of tortillas, tamales, and countless other foods. For vegetables, the trinity of tomatoes, onions, and peppers can always be found in any kitchen. Rice and beans are also fundamental to forming a complete plate, regardless of what stew or main dish you are making. A well-stocked Mexican kitchen will also need cooking oils, flours, cheeses, herbs and spices, and, let's not forget, dried peppers, which play a major role in adding flavor to a lot of Mexican recipes.

Below you will find a list of essential ingredients that are commonly kept in the pantry and refrigerator of the standard Mexican kitchen. The majority of these will be used to make the recipes in this book. Although there are a few items that aren't always stocked in kitchens (as they can be seasonal or regional), they are still ingredients that are commonplace in our cuisine.

FRUITS AND VEGETABLES

AVOCADOS: Avocados are used for making guacamole and for garnishing lots of other dishes, such as Ceviche (page 134), Coctel de Camarón (page 137), antojitos, soups, and salsas. Regardless of what they are eating, most Mexicans will love to have an avocado on the table to accompany their meal in some way. To make sure you select perfectly ripe avocados, look for those that have a dark green color. The skin should give a little when you gently press it. If an avocado is too firm, it means it's not ripe yet; if it feels mushy, it means the avocado is past its prime. In my kitchen, I usually have two or three avocados at different stages of ripeness and consume them as they become ripe. If you want to accelerate the ripening process, you can wrap the avocados in paper (brown paper bag, newspaper, etc.) and store them in a dark, dry place for a couple days.

BANANAS: Bananas are the most consumed fruit in Mexico and are enjoyed by themselves or in smoothies and milkshakes, with the most popular being the banana milkshake, a common breakfast drink made with bananas, milk, sugar, ice, and vanilla extract.

CABBAGE: A green/white cabbage (*col blanca*) is commonly found in some soups, but it is also used in salads and as a garnish for tacos and other antojitos. Shredded cabbage can be substituted with shredded lettuce when used as a garnish.

CARROTS: Carrots are used in soups, stews, salads, and other dishes. In addition to being cooked, carrots are also pickled with jalapeños (page 184) and are sold like this in cans and jars at many grocery stores.

CHAYOTES: Chayotes are a type of pear-shaped gourd that is commonly used in soups and stews. They are light green in color and 5 to 6 inches (12.5 to 15 cm) long. Chayotes can also be steamed and served as a side dish. You can find them at Latin and Asian stores.

CORN (FRESH): The fresh corn used in Mexico is not as sweet as the corn found in the United States. The recipes in this book are adapted to the corn you can buy in the US.

GARLIC: This is an everyday ingredient that is used in almost any dish, including rice, beans, stews, soups, and more.

LIMES: Limes are used in a variety of ways in Mexico. Their juices are squeezed on top of foods such as tacos, soups, and even fresh fruit cocktails. Lime juice can also be used when marinating meat and seafood.

MANGOES: As a major producer of this fruit, Mexico boasts a wide variety of mangoes, with the most popular type being the Ataulfo mango. Mangoes can be used to make juices, *aguas frescas*, desserts, and ice creams. They are also sold by street vendors, fresh and peeled as snacks (most people like to top them with chili powder).

NOPALES: Nopales (cactus paddles) have a neutral flavor and a texture slightly similar to that of okra or green beans. A versatile vegetable, nopales are used in a variety of ways in Mexican cooking, including in salads (page 170), soups, stews, and juices (page 224). They can be cooked on the grill to accompany meats or chopped and scrambled with eggs (page 31) for breakfast. Besides being versatile, nopales are also rich in fiber, vitamins, and other important nutrients. To prepare nopales, first trim off the edges using a sharp knife, then scrape all the spines off the surface of the paddle. Do this by running your knife from the bottom of the paddle to the top (the rounder part) until the surface is completely clean. (At first, use kitchen tongs or gloves to protect your hands from the spines until you're comfortable cleaning them.) Rinse the pads, pat them dry, and then cut them into smaller pieces for cooking. You can find nopales at most Latin stores and in some chain supermarkets. At Latin stores, you can find them sold already cleaned (with the spines removed), and sometimes even diced. If you can't find fresh nopales, you can use the ones sold in a jar.

ONIONS: White onions are the main type of onion used for almost any dish throughout Mexico, with the exception of the Yucatán Peninsula, where red onions are an important part of the local cuisine and are commonly used in addition to white onions. Green onions are also used throughout the country, especially when grilling meats.

ORANGES: Mexicans love having freshly squeezed orange juice in the morning, but that's not the only way oranges are consumed. They are used to make aguas frescas, cocktails, preserves, and even atoles (page 227). A few dishes and marinades use oranges (or bitter oranges) to tenderize meat and add flavor.

PINEAPPLES: Pineapples can be used to make fruit salads, preserves, and desserts, as well as a variety of drinks, including juices, aguas frescas, cocktails, and Tepache (page 228).

PLANTAINS: Plantains are more commonly found in the coastal and southern regions of Mexico. Although plantains are used in some soups and stews in the south of Mexico, they are primarily fried and served as a side dish for some regional dishes. Plátanos Fritos (page 174) can also be enjoyed as a delicious stand-alone dessert (either sliced or whole).

POTATOES: White potatoes are one of the most common varieties of potato in Mexico and are used in lots of Mexican dishes. You can also use golden or red potatoes.

SQUASH (AND/OR ZUCCHINI): Mexican squash (light green in color with an elongated shape) is slightly sweeter than the common zucchini found in the United States. Mexican squash can be found in Latin stores and some Asian markets.

Nowadays, you can find the two types at Latin stores: the elongated type and the small, round ones. If you can't find them, you can always use zucchini as a substitute.

STRAWBERRIES: Strawberries are used to make drinks, preserves, and desserts, such as Rollo de Fresa (page 194). One of the most common ways people consume fresh strawberries in Mexico is by making *fresas con crema* (strawberries with cream). This quick treat can be prepared by combining sliced strawberries, sour cream (or Mexican crema), and sugar.

TOMATILLOS: Tomatillos can be used in raw or cooked form to make salsas, and they are also a component in many stews. Larger tomatillos tend to be bitter, so choose the smaller ones.

TOMATOES: Most of the recipes in this book use Roma or plum tomatoes, but you can also use beefsteak tomatoes. All are great for salsas and stews. Allow the tomatoes to completely ripen before using them, as they will become juicier and add more color to your dishes. I usually place them in a basket for a few days near my kitchen window until they ripen, before placing them in the fridge.

PEPPERS

ANCHO PEPPERS (DRIED): Ancho peppers are wrinkly peppers with a dark burgundy color. When buying dried peppers, make sure they are still pliable; if they are too stiff and crumble easily, this means that they are old. While ancho peppers are used in salsas, they are mostly used in stews and soups. The chile mulato is related to the ancho but has a darker chocolate color. Mulato peppers are used to make mole poblano along with ancho and pasilla peppers.

ÁRBOL PEPPERS (DRIED): The árbol is a spicy pepper with a long, skinny body, a thin skin, and an orangey-red color. They are used to add heat to stews and salsas. The seeds and veins are usually not removed when cooking it. The árbol pepper is one of the most commonly available hot peppers at Latin markets. Its intense heat and versatility make it a favorite choice for spicing up a wide range of dishes. When buying árbol peppers, make sure they have stems and are fluffy, not flat.

CHIPOTLE PEPPERS (DRIED): The chipotle pepper is actually a jalapeño pepper that has been left to mature on the plant until it has a deep red color, and then it is subjected to a smoking process until it's dehydrated. Chipotle peppers are used in stews and salsas.

GUAJILLO PEPPERS (DRIED): Guajillo peppers are peppers with a smooth and shiny skin. They are not hot but still add a lot of flavor to soups and stews.

HABANERO PEPPERS: Recognized as one of the hottest peppers on Earth, the habanero is a staple food in the Yucatán Peninsula, where it is used practically every day. It is primarily used to make salsas, pickles, and other condiments, which serve as excellent complements for dishes such as Cochinita Pibil (page 113).

JALAPEÑO PEPPERS: Jalapeños can be used to make both raw and cooked salsas. They are also used in some *guisados* (stews). Not all jalapeño peppers have the same spiciness, so if you like them to be spicy, look for the ones that have lots of veins on the skin.

MORITA PEPPERS (DRIED): The morita pepper is a dried hot pepper that is primarily used to prepare salsas, stews, and some regional dishes. It has some similarities with chipotle peppers, but there are a few distinctions to keep in mind: the morita pepper is smaller and has a darker, shinier skin, as well as a slightly sweeter taste (while still delivering a spicy kick). They are also known as *chipotle mora, chipotle negro,* and *chile seco*. In case you can't find morita peppers, chipotle peppers are a fitting alternative.

PASILLA PEPPERS (DRIED): Pasilla peppers are long and wrinkly with a deep, dark brown color. They are a mild type of pepper used for stews and salsas.

PIQUÍN PEPPERS: Despite being some of the smallest peppers you will find, piquín peppers hold a lot of heat. In dried form, this pepper is often crushed and sprinkled on fresh fruit, cocktails, and soups. Piquín peppers can also be cooked, toasted, or crushed to make salsas and stews. Fresh ones are often ground in a molcajete to make fresh salsas. You can find them in Latin stores and online.

POBLANO PEPPERS: Poblano peppers have a dark green color, fleshy skin, and a conical shape, measuring an average of 5 inches (12.5 cm) in length. They are usually mild in spiciness. Poblano peppers can be stuffed with fillings such as meat or cheese (*chiles rellenos*), or they can be cut into strips and added to dishes such as stews or tamales (strips of poblanos are commonly referred to as *rajas*, which means "strips"). Poblanos are also used in Espagueti Verde (page 144). For a better flavor, look for poblanos sold at farmers' markets.

SERRANO PEPPERS: Though not as popular outside of Mexico as jalapeño peppers, you can use serranos in the same way as jalapeños in salsas or stews. Serranos are smaller, but spicier, than jalapeños, and the spiciness of serranos will vary depending on the region where they are grown.

HERBS AND SPICES

BAY LEAVES (DRIED): Many cooks like to add one or two bay leaves to the water when they cook pork or beef. They are also used to prepare stews and when pickling peppers.

BLACK PEPPERCORNS: Whole black peppercorns are ground using a molcajete or a spice grinder. Using freshly ground pepper is the best choice when making Mexican food, but you can also use ground black pepper.

CILANTRO (FRESH): Cilantro is used as an ingredient in salsas and stews, as well as a garnish for many dishes. To keep it fresh longer, wrap it in aluminum foil and place it inside a plastic bag in your refrigerator.

CUMIN (DRIED): You can use ground cumin or grind your own seeds at home in a molcajete or spice grinder (freshly ground is better). While cumin is a common ingredient in the cuisines of border states like Tamaulipas, Nuevo Leon, and Coahuila, it is used more sparingly in other regions of the country.

EPAZOTE (FRESH): Epazote is commonly used when cooking black beans. It is also used for some stews, soups, and corn-tortilla quesadillas, as well as for Chilaquiles (page 34). If you can't find fresh epazote, you can find the dried leaves online. They won't have the same pungent taste epazote is known for, but they will still work. If you're able to find fresh epazote, you can preserve it by freezing it in freezer bags for up to 3 months.

MARJORAM (DRIED): In Mexican cooking, marjoram is often used with thyme and bay leaf to form a trinity of herbs used in a lot of stews and pickles. Some people also use these herbs in recipes for making sausage and chorizo.

MEXICAN CINNAMON (STICKS): Mexican cinnamon has a sweeter and more complex flavor compared to other cinnamon varieties, as well as a thinner and softer bark. It has many uses in Mexican cuisine, from desserts and drinks to even some stews, so it's always good to keep some in your pantry. Mexican cinnamon sticks can be found in Latin markets and online.

MEXICAN OREGANO (DRIED): Make sure to use Mexican oregano when cooking Mexican dishes, as its taste is quite different from the Italian and Greek oreganos. You can find it at Latin stores, specialty stores, and online.

MINT (FRESH): Mint (and spearmint) is used in some soups and stews and can also be mixed with fruits to make aguas frescas. It is also used to prepare tea.

PARSLEY (FRESH): Parsley is used as an ingredient in some soups and stews. It is also used for garnishing many dishes.

THYME (DRIED): Dried thyme is commonly added to stews and is also used when pickling vegetables and peppers.

DRY INGREDIENTS

ACHIOTE (ANNATTO) PASTE: Achiote paste is made out of annatto seeds and a variety of other spices. Known for its impressive flavor and its orange-y-red color, this paste is used to make many dishes from the Yucatán region, including the famous Cochinita Pibil (page 113) and Pollo Pibil (page 111). Some popular brands of achiote paste are La Anita and El Yucateco.

ALL-PURPOSE FLOUR: For the best results when making flour tortillas or baked goods, choose a good-quality all-purpose flour. If you're baking bread that uses yeast, it is recommended to use bread flour to guarantee better results.

BANANA LEAVES: Banana leaves are used to wrap tamales in the southern and coastal regions of the country. They are also used to wrap fish and meats to steam or bake them. You can find fresh banana leaves in Latin and Asian grocery stores. You can also find them frozen, even in some regular grocery stores; they will need to be thawed first. Here's how to prep banana leaves before using them: Cut the banana leaves into square sections, about 10 to 12 inches (25 to 30 cm) wide. Briefly pass the banana leaf pieces over the flame of your stove, making sure to pass the whole leaf over the flame. The texture of the leaf will become soft and pliable with the heat, and its surface will turn glossy. Afterward, rinse the leaf sections with warm water and dry them with a kitchen towel.

BEANS: Although there are many varieties of beans in Mexico, black beans and pinto beans are the most popular. Pinto beans are more common in the northern states, whereas black beans are used in the rest of the country. I always have both in my pantry and recommend you do the same. Cooked beans can be stored in the freezer for up to 2 months.

CHICKEN BOUILLON: Available in cubes and as a powder, chicken bouillon is a common ingredient in Mexican homes. People mix it with water to use as a substitute for chicken broth in many recipes, including soups and stews. You can use this substitution for the recipes in this book.

CORN HUSKS: You will use many corn husks when making tamales. When buying corn husks, check them to make sure they look clean, are the same size, and are still soft (not too dry or crunchy).

CORN TORTILLAS: If you don't have time to make your own tortillas, look for those sold at Latin stores or tortilla factories (*tortillerias*). Store-bought tortillas can freeze well for a couple of months when wrapped tightly in a freezer bag.

FLOUR TORTILLAS: Flour tortillas are not everyday fare in many regions of Mexico, as they are only popular in the northern states. Nowadays, you can find cooked flour tortillas at most grocery stores, but I personally love making my own at home.

LONG-GRAIN WHITE RICE: Long-grain white rice has less starch content than medium-grain rice, rendering a fluffy rice that won't stick together.

MASA HARINA: When fresh corn dough (*masa*) is not available, masa harina is the flour that is used to make tortillas and several other Mexican foods (*masa* means "dough" and *harina* means "flour"). To produce masa harina, corn is first cooked in limewater in a process called nixtamalization, and then it is dried and ground into a fine powder. While masa harina is sometimes referred to as "corn flour," it is important to not confuse it with regular corn flour, which does not use nixtamalized corn and is generally not ground as fine as masa harina is. If you are looking to buy this flour, make sure that the package says "masa harina" on it. You can find masa harina sold in Latin stores, and nowadays, a lot of grocery stores in the United States carry it is as well. The most common brand is Maseca, but there are other options available as well, including some organic brands.

MEXICAN CHOCOLATE TABLETS: These chocolate tablets are commonly sold in a box containing six round tablets, each weighing about 3.2 ounces (90 g). The most popular brand is Abuelita (by Nestlé), with the second most common brand being Ibarra. These days, there are many other brands of Mexican chocolate, including some sourced from the state of Oaxaca. If you cannot find Mexican chocolate tablets in your supermarket, you can easily buy them online.

PILONCILLO: Piloncillo is a type of raw sugar that comes in a cone shape. It boasts a dark brown color and an aromatic flavor similar to molasses. When buying piloncillo (also called *panela*, but not to be confused with queso panela), make sure to look for the pure version, which has a dark color. Some stores carry a look-alike version that is just plain sugar in a cone shape, lacking the flavor and nutrients of real piloncillo. If you have a hard time cutting the piloncillo for the amount needed, place it in the microwave for intervals of 30 seconds until it is softened enough to cut. Be careful when taking it out of the microwave because it can get extremely hot.

DAIRY

MEXICAN CREMA: Mexican crema, or cream, is mostly used as a topping, drizzled on tostadas, crispy tacos, sopes, and other antojitos. It also used in soups, stews, and dishes such as Espegueti Verde (page 144) to add some creaminess. Mexican crema is available at most supermarkets. If you can't find crema, you can substitute it with a mixture of equal parts heavy cream and sour cream. Alternatively, you can use sour cream or slightly dilute cream cheese with whole milk to create the texture of the Mexican crema.

QUESO COTIJA: Like Mexican crema, queso Cotija is commonly used to top enchiladas and antojitos. It can be substituted with crumbled queso fresco or, as a last resort, Parmesan cheese.

QUESO FRESCO: Usually sold in a round wheel in a plastic pouch or plastic container, queso fresco is perfect to use crumbled over refried beans, enchiladas, and more. You can use feta cheese if you can't find queso fresco, but keep in mind that feta is a saltier cheese.

QUESO OAXACA: Queso Oaxaca is often used as a filling for foods such as quesadillas, tamales, and chiles rellenos. It is also used to make Queso Fundido (page 165). Fresh mozzarella cheese is a good substitute, as are other melting cheeses, such as Monterey Jack or Muenster.

QUESO PANELA: The texture of queso panela is somewhat spongy and not as crumbly as queso fresco. Besides being used as a garnish for antojitos, queso panela is also served diced in soups such as Caldo Tlalpeño (page 78). If you can't find queso panela, you can use queso fresco instead.

CANNED GOODS

CHIPOTLE PEPPERS IN ADOBO SAUCE:
Chipotle peppers in adobo sauce are used to add flavor to dishes such as Caldo de Camarón (page 74) and Creamy Chipotle Chicken (page 102). Generally, only one or two peppers are used in a recipe, so once you open a can, save the remaining peppers in a container in your refrigerator.

CONDENSED MILK: Condensed milk is a staple in Mexican homes, and is used in a variety of sweet foods, including iconic desserts such as pastel de tres leches and flan. It is also drizzled on Plátanos Fritos (page 174) and fruits, like fresh strawberries, as well as being mixed into drinks, including coffee and even horchata.

PICKLED JALAPEÑOS AND CARROTS:
Pickled jalapeños and carrots are often served as an accompaniment to meals like stews or sandwiches. Besides being sold in cans, they are also available in jars. You can also easily make them at home (page 184).

FATS AND MEAT

CHORIZO: Mexican chorizo is made out of ground pork, vinegar, and a mixture of spices and dried peppers. It goes through a short curing period, but it is not dried until hard like its Spanish counterpart. Mexican chorizo is soft and can be crumbled when cooking it in a pan to make dishes such as Huevos con Chorizo (page 27) and Papas con Chorizo (page 44). In the United States, a lot of grocery stores will sell some sort of packaged chorizo, and certain Latin stores will sell fresh chorizo if they have a butchery section. When buying chorizo, choose one that has coarse-ground meat. If the chorizo doesn't render enough fat (1 to 2 tablespoons) while cooking it, you will need to add vegetable oil to the pan.

LARD: Lard plays an important role in enhancing the flavors of certain dishes, including stews, tacos, and even refried beans. It's an essential component of the dough used for making tamales, and you can also find it in the dough for some antojitos, which can also be fried in lard. You can find lard being sold at large Latin stores that have a butcher section.

OLIVE OIL: Traditionally, Spanish olive oil was used for preparing Mexican dishes with Spanish influence, such as Beef Shank Stew (page 90) and Tilapia a la Veracruzana (page 130). But nowadays, Italian olive oil is becoming more popular and being used in a larger variety of dishes. Olive oil is also commonly used in salads.

SHORTENING: Shortening is mainly used for baking cookies, breads, and other pastries.

VEGETABLE OIL: Vegetable oil is an essential ingredient that is used in the kitchen almost every day. It is used for cooking rice, stews, and even eggs for breakfast.

TOOLS & EQUIPMENT

All the recipes featured in this book can be prepared using common tools and equipment that you already have in your kitchen; however, if you find yourself cooking Mexican food frequently, you may want to invest in some more traditional Mexican kitchen items. Here is a list of the tools, cookware, and equipment that are most commonly used in a Mexican household.

BEAN MASHER: There are two types of bean mashers: those made with wood and those made with metal. Wooden bean mashers have a flat surface for mashing the beans, while the metal ones have holes in them, similar to a potato masher. If you don't have a bean masher, you can use a potato masher to mash your beans. Alternatively, you can use a glass cup that has a thick, heavy bottom.

CAZUELA: The cazuela is a traditional Mexican clay pot. It is convenient to have cazuelas of different sizes and shapes, with lids (especially with vent holes). I recommend having a small cazuela (around 8 inches/20 cm) for cooking rice, and a medium-size one (10 to 12 inches/20 to 25 cm) for making stews. A clay pot is also highly recommended for cooking beans and lentil soups because the clay truly enhances the flavor of your food.

CLOTH NAPKINS OR KITCHEN TOWELS: When tortillas are made, they are wrapped in a cloth napkin before being placed inside a tortilla basket. This is done to help keep them warm. In addition to being used when serving tortillas, cloth napkins are also used to line the bread baskets when serving bread, such as Bolillos (page 215). Cloth napkins and kitchen towels are also used for covering doughs, either for rising or for keeping them moist (as is the case for corn masa dough).

COMAL: A comal is a round griddle, usually with a small ridge around the edge. It is commonly used for making and reheating tortillas and toasting seeds, peppers, and vegetables for salsas, as well as for reheating foods such as tamales and empanadas. The earliest comals were made out of clay, but nowadays, most people use a comal made out of stainless steel, cast iron, or a nonstick material. A griddle, skillet, or crepe pan (all preferably nonstick) is a good substitute for a comal.

FREEZER BAGS (LARGE): Freezer bags are not only useful for storing extra tamales, empanadas, beans, and any leftovers in the freezer, but they are my personal choice for making corn tortillas, Empanadas (page 127), Gorditas (page 53), and Sopes (page 55). For this purpose, cut two 7 x 7-inch (18 x 18 cm) plastic sheets from one resealable freezer bag, and then place a dough ball between them before pressing in a tortilla press or with a glass pie dish.

MOLCAJETE: A molcajete is a special mortar (with its accompanying pestle) that is made out of lava rock and has a very coarse, porous surface. Molcajetes are good for grinding spices as well as for making and serving salsas and guacamole, giving you the best control over the texture of the ingredients.

MOLINILLO: The molinillo, a traditional wooden whisk, has been a beloved tool for making *chocolate caliente* (Mexican hot chocolate) since colonial times, around the 1700s. Crafted from a single piece of turned wood, it features two rings encircling a striated and hollow sphere at the lower part. To froth your hot chocolate, simply submerge the head of the molinillo in the chocolate and rotate it back and forth by rubbing the handle between your hands. This twisting motion will generate foam, resulting in a delightfully frothy hot chocolate.

ROLLING PIN: In Mexican cuisine, a rolling pin is mostly used for making flour tortillas. Due to its gluten content, the dough for flour tortillas tends to shrink back when stretched, making a tortilla press unsuitable for making flour tortillas. Additionally, rolling pins are used for making cookies and piecrusts.

TAMALERA: A tamalera is a large pot with a steam rack at the bottom. As its name implies, it is used to cook tamales, but it can also be used to make certain steamed meats. If you're making tamales

and don't have a tamalera, you can improvise by using one of these methods: you can crumble up some aluminum foil and place it in the bottom of a pot, then cover it with corn husks and place the tamales on top, or you can cut some holes in a disposable aluminum pie dish, then place it upside down in the pot to use it as a steam rack.

TORTILLA BASKET: The tortilla basket is a common sight in many Mexican households. They are made with natural fibers and are used to keep tortillas (wrapped in cloth napkins) warm at the table. They are also a great way to decorate your table setting.

TORTILLA PRESS: A tortilla press is used for making corn tortillas and other foods that use corn masa, such as Gorditas (page 53), Sopes (page 55), and Empanadas (page 127). Tortilla presses are traditionally made from wood or cast iron, but they are also being made out of other materials these days. In case you don't have access to a tortilla press, a very effective method that I recommend is using a glass pie dish to form the tortillas. You would still place the ball of dough between two sheets of plastic cut from a freezer bag, but instead of pressing it between the two plates of the tortilla press, you would press it down on your work surface using the bottom of the pie dish. A benefit of using this method is that you can see the tortilla being formed through the glass as you press down on the pie dish, making sure that it has reached the desired diameter and thickness.

WOODEN SPOONS: My most-used utensils, wooden spoons can be used when making stews, beans, and rice. Unlike their metal counterparts, wooden spoons help protect your pots and pans from being scratched or damaged.

BREAKFASTS

HUEVOS A LA MEXICANA

Mexican-Style Eggs

This is an extremely well-known breakfast dish, both in restaurants and in people's homes. Besides being tasty and wholesome, its popularity may also be because it's very simple to make and requires only a few ingredients. Almost everyone has eggs, tomatoes, onions, and peppers in their kitchen, making this an accessible recipe for all. In Mexico, we often refer to something in its diminutive form as a way to add a little love to it. Food is no exception to this, so we commonly refer to this dish as *huevitos a la Mexicana*.

PREP TIME: 8 minutes	**COOK TIME:** 9 minutes	**YIELD:** 2 servings

1 tablespoon vegetable oil

¼ cup (35 g) chopped white onion

1 serrano pepper (see Notas), finely chopped

2 plum tomatoes, diced

4 large eggs

Salt

FOR GARNISHING AND SERVING

1 cup (240 g) refried beans (black or pinto)

Sliced or crumbed queso fresco (optional)

4 to 6 tortilla chips (optional)

4 warm corn tortillas

1. In a medium skillet (see Notas), heat the oil over medium-high heat. Add the onion and cook for about 1 minute. Add the serrano pepper, stir, and cook for 2 more minutes. Add the tomatoes, stir, and cook for another 2 minutes. Make sure to not overcook the vegetables.

2. While the vegetables are cooking, crack the eggs into a medium bowl and lightly beat them.

3. Pour the beaten eggs over the vegetables in the skillet and season with salt. Let them cook for about 2 minutes, then gently stir the vegetables into the eggs—don't mix them too much; the eggs should still have some large curdles in them. Cook for 2 more minutes, or until the egg whites are set, then promptly remove the skillet from the heat. Do not overcook the eggs.

4. If using, garnish the refried beans with the cheese and/or tortilla chips, then serve with the eggs and tortillas.

NOTAS

* *If you can't find serrano peppers, use jalapeño peppers or any other type of pepper available. You can also increase the number of peppers if you want this dish to be spicy. I like to add some extra raw slices of serrano pepper to my eggs.*

* *I prefer to use a nonstick frying pan for this recipe.*

* *The coarse and homely aspect of the eggs is part of the beauty of this dish.*

HUEVOS RANCHEROS

A simple and beautiful dish, *huevos rancheros* is a classic Mexican breakfast that has won the hearts of diners far beyond Mexico's borders. You can find it on the menus of Mexican and Tex-Mex restaurants all over the United States, as well as in restaurants that don't even specialize in Mexican food. In Mexico, huevos rancheros are enjoyed both in restaurants and in people's homes—from the big, bustling cities to small, faraway villages.

PREP TIME: 20 minutes	**COOK TIME:** 30 minutes	**YIELD:** 2 servings

SALSA

2 plum tomatoes

1 small clove garlic

1 jalapeño or serrano pepper

1 slice medium onion (about ⅓ inch/ 8.5 mm thick)

1 tablespoon vegetable oil

Salt

HUEVOS RANCHEROS

¼ cup (60 ml) vegetable oil

4 medium corn tortillas

4 large eggs

½ cup (120 g) refried black beans, warmed

Salt

NOTAS

* *The salsa can also be made by roasting the ingredients.*
* *You can garnish huevos rancheros with avocado slices, fresh cilantro, chopped onions, and/or a sprinkle of crumbled queso fresco and serve with a side of warm refried beans.*

1. To make the salsa: Place the tomatoes, garlic, pepper, and onion slice in a medium saucepan and cover with water. Place the saucepan over medium-high heat. When the water comes to a boil, reduce the heat to medium-low and simmer until the tomatoes and the pepper are cooked, about 15 minutes.

2. Remove the saucepan from the heat and carefully transfer the cooked ingredients to a blender along with ¼ cup (60 ml) of the cooking water. Process until smooth.

3. In a small skillet, heat the 1 tablespoon oil over medium-low heat. Pour the salsa into the pan and cook until it starts to boil, 4 to 5 minutes. Promptly remove the pan from the heat. Season the salsa with salt.

4. To make the huevos rancheros: In a separate small skillet, heat the ¼ cup (60 ml) oil over medium-high heat. Once the oil is hot, lightly fry the corn tortillas, one at a time, turning them once until they become soft and pliable but not crispy, about 30 seconds per side. Transfer the fried tortillas to a paper towel–lined plate to absorb any excess oil. Place the tortillas near the stove to keep them warm while you fry the eggs.

5. In the same skillet over medium-high heat, fry the eggs to your liking (sunny-side up, over easy, basted, etc.). Season with salt.

6. To assemble the dish, place 2 corn tortillas, slightly overlapping each other, on a plate. Spread about 2 tablespoons of the refried beans on each tortilla, then carefully slide 2 cooked eggs on top.

7. Spoon a generous amount of the salsa over the eggs and serve with extra garnishes, if desired (see Notas).

HUEVOS CON CHORIZO

Chorizo and Eggs

Huevos con chorizo (also called *chorizo con huevos*) is one of the most popular ways that chorizo is enjoyed for breakfast in Mexico. It is extremely easy to prepare, making it one of the most useful dishes you can learn to cook. It is a classic recipe that I'm sure will come in handy on those busy mornings when you need a quick breakfast that everyone will love.

PREP TIME: 5 minutes	COOK TIME: 10 minutes	YIELD: 2 servings

6 ounces (170 g) Mexican chorizo (about 2 medium-size chorizo links), casings removed

4 large eggs

Salt

FOR SERVING

Refried beans (black or pinto)

Sliced avocado

Warm corn or flour tortillas

1. Heat a medium skillet over medium-high heat. While the pan is preheating, crumble the chorizo into a bowl—this will help it cook evenly. Add the crumbled chorizo to the hot pan and cook for about 5 minutes. If there are larger pieces of chorizo, break them apart with a wooden spoon to make them smaller. (Alternatively, you can leave the chorizo whole and break it up in the pan as it cooks.)

2. Once the chorizo is cooked, crack the eggs into the pan, but do not stir. Season the eggs and chorizo with a little salt. Wait for about 1 minute, then proceed to scramble the eggs, gently stirring them to combine them with the chorizo. Keep cooking and stirring until the eggs are done to your liking (see Notas).

3. Serve with refried beans, avocado slices, and tortillas.

NOTAS

✖ *I like my eggs cooked tender—slightly soft, but still cooked (without being wet)—which takes less than 2 minutes.*

✖ *You can make some delicious breakfast burritos with this dish, when served with refried beans and flour tortillas. You can also make tortas using sandwich bread or Bolillos (page 215). Spread some warmed refried beans or mayonnaise on the inside of the bread slices.*

HUEVOS EN SALSA

Scrambled Eggs with Salsa

Huevos en salsa, also known as chile huevillo, is a humble yet heartwarming dish. I learned to make it from my grandma at her ranch in Veracruz. She would prepare tacos with this as the filling for the men in the family who were working in the sugarcane fields. Huevos en salsa is a classic breakfast that has surely been made in pretty much every Mexican household, and you can also find it on the menu at many Mexican restaurants and diners that serve a breakfast course. It is usually served with a side of refried beans and some warm tortillas. This recipe uses a red salsa, which is most common for this dish, but you can find huevos en salsa made with a green salsa too. You can also make it using a salsa made with dried peppers, such as guajillo. In certain parts of the country, this dish is known as *chile huevillo*.

PREP TIME: 10 minutes	**COOK TIME:** 25 minutes	**YIELD:** 2 servings

SALSA

3 plum tomatoes

1 jalapeño pepper or 2 serrano peppers

1 small clove garlic

Salt

SCRAMBLED EGGS

1 tablespoon vegetable oil

¼ cup (35 g) chopped white onion

4 eggs

Salt

FOR SERVING

Refried beans (black or pinto)

Sliced or crumbled queso fresco

Warm corn tortillas

Avocado slices (optional)

NOTA *I prefer to pan-scramble my eggs, but if you would rather beat them in a bowl before cooking them, that is okay too.*

1. To make the salsa: Place the tomatoes, pepper, and garlic in a medium saucepan and cover with water. Cook over medium-high heat until the tomatoes and pepper are cooked, 16 to 18 minutes.

2. Carefully transfer the cooked ingredients to a blender along with ⅓ cup (80 ml) of the cooking water, and process until smooth. Season with salt.

3. To make the scrambled eggs: In a medium skillet, heat the oil over medium heat. Add the onion and cook and stir until it becomes transparent, about 2 minutes. Crack the eggs into the pan and season with salt (see Nota). Cook, stirring gently, for about 3 minutes, or until they are tender or well done (depending on your taste). Once the eggs are cooked, transfer them to a bowl.

4. Wipe down the skillet with a paper towel and place it back on the stove over medium heat. Add the salsa and warm for 2 to 3 minutes. Add the scrambled eggs for just enough time to warm them again, mixing gently so that the eggs are completely covered in the salsa.

5. Garnish the refried beans with the cheese, then serve with the eggs, tortillas, and avocado (if using).

NOPALES CON HUEVO

Cactus Paddles and Eggs

Nopales with eggs is a nutritious option for a quick breakfast (and it's vegetarian too). For some reason, my mom never prepared nopales this way; it wasn't until I was married that I started to cook them like this, because that's how my husband enjoys them. We like to serve them with warm bolillos and a side of beans (either out of the pot or refried). Sometimes my husband will make a torta with this dish and refried beans.

PREP TIME: 4 minutes	**COOK TIME:** 6 minutes	**YIELD:** 2 servings

1 tablespoon vegetable oil

2 tablespoons chopped green onion

1 cup (150 g) cleaned, diced, and cooked nopales (see page 11 for nopales prep and the Nota for cooking instructions)

4 large eggs

Salt

FOR SERVING

Beans from the pot or refried beans (black or pinto)

Warm Bolillos (page 215) or corn tortillas

1. In a large skillet, heat the oil over medium-high heat. Add the green onion and cook and stir for 1 minute.

2. Stir in the nopales and cook for 2 minutes. Add the eggs and cook until tender, stirring as needed. Season with salt.

3. Serve with beans and bolillos or tortillas.

NOTA *Here is an easy way to cook nopales for this recipe: Place the diced nopales in a medium skillet and add just enough water to cover them. Place the skillet over medium-high heat, simmer for 7 to 8 minutes, and then drain the water. Return the pan to the stove, add the oil and chopped green onion, then follow the recipe steps above.*

MACHACA CON HUEVO

Machaca and Eggs

Machaca con huevo is a popular dish in the northern states of Mexico, especially at breakfast or brunch. It is almost always served with a side of pinto beans and some flour tortillas. When you visit cities such as Monterrey in the state of Nuevo León, this dish is bound to be on the menus of the local restaurants. *Machaca* is a type of dried beef that's popular in northern Mexico, and although machaca con huevo is the most common way to prepare it, it can also be used in soups or cooked in a salsa. Machaca and eggs also makes a great filling for burritos.

PREP TIME: 10 minutes	**COOK TIME:** 15 minutes	**YIELD:** 4 servings

2 tablespoons vegetable oil

½ cup (70 g) finely chopped white onion

1 cup (100 g) finely shredded machaca (see Notas)

1 cup (180 g) finely chopped plum tomato

2 serrano peppers, finely chopped

6 large eggs, lightly beaten

Salt

FOR SERVING

Refried pinto beans

Sliced or crumbled queso fresco

Warm corn tortillas

Spicy salsa of choice

Avocado slices (optional)

1. In a medium skillet, heat the oil over medium-high heat. Add the onion and cook and stir until translucent, about 3 minutes, then add the machaca; it will absorb the oil in the skillet. Reduce the heat to medium, and cook the machaca for about 5 minutes, stirring frequently and letting it brown a little.

2. Add the tomato and serrano peppers to the skillet and cook, stirring occasionally, for another 8 minutes. By now the tomatoes will have released their juices.

3. Reduce the heat to low, then pour the eggs into the skillet and cook, stirring as needed, until they are cooked to your liking. (Do not cook the eggs for too long or they will be dry.) Season with salt. Machaca is usually salty, so taste it first before adding more salt.

4. Garnish the refried beans with the cheese, then serve with the eggs, tortillas, salsa, and avocado (if using).

NOTAS

✳ *You can find machaca from Mexico in Latin stores or online. If you can't find machaca, it can be substituted with shredded cooked beef.*

✳ *If you like garlic, add 1 clove, finely chopped, in step 1.*

CHILAQUILES

There are many classic and beloved Mexican breakfast recipes, but *chilaquiles* are in a league of their own. A dish loved by everyone, chilaquiles can be found pretty much anywhere in Mexico, from mom-and-pop diners to chain restaurants and even five-star hotels. A plate of chilaquiles is quite simple: fried tortilla chips covered in a red or green salsa (red in the case of this recipe) and usually garnished with crumbled cheese and a drizzle of crema. Besides the usual garnishes, chilaquiles can also be topped with a fried egg or some shredded chicken.

PREP TIME: 10 minutes	**COOK TIME:** 30 minutes	**YIELD:** 4 servings

SALSA

4 large plum tomatoes

1 large clove garlic

2 serrano peppers (see Notas)

1 thick slice medium white onion

1 tablespoon vegetable oil

Salt

CHILAQUILES

¼ cup (60 ml) vegetable oil, plus more if needed

8 corn tortillas (preferably day-old), cut into 8 triangles each

2 fresh epazote leaves (or ¼ teaspoon dried epazote) (optional)

Salt and black pepper

FOR GARNISHING AND SERVING

¾ cup (90 g) crumbled queso fresco

½ cup (120 ml) Mexican crema or sour cream

1 medium avocado, sliced

⅛ red onion, thinly sliced (optional)

1 tablespoon fresh cilantro leaves (optional)

Refried beans (black or pinto) (optional)

1. To make the salsa: Place the tomatoes, garlic, serrano peppers, and onion slice in a medium saucepan and cover with water. Bring the water to a boil over medium-high heat. Once boiling, reduce the heat and let simmer for 12 to 15 minutes, until the tomatoes, garlic, peppers, and onion are soft and tender. Carefully transfer the cooked ingredients to a blender along with ¼ cup (60 ml) of the cooking water and process until smooth. Season with salt.

2. To make the chilaquiles: In a large skillet, heat the ¼ cup (60 ml) oil over medium-high heat. Fry the tortilla triangles until golden and crisp. (You may need to work in 2 or 3 batches to avoid overcrowding the skillet, adding more oil as needed.) Using a slotted spoon, drain the fried tortillas and transfer them to a paper towel–lined plate to absorb any excess oil.

3. Wipe down the skillet with a paper towel, then place it over medium heat and add the 1 tablespoon oil. Add the salsa to the pan. Once it comes to a boil, reduce the heat, add the epazote leaves (if using), and cook for 5 minutes. Season with salt and black pepper.

4. Carefully stir the fried tortillas into the sauce but avoid breaking them. Cook for 2 minutes for crispy chilaquiles and for 3 minutes for a softer texture.

5. Garnish with the crumbled cheese, crema, avocado slices, onion slices (if using), and cilantro (if using). Serve immediately (to preserve their crispiness) alongside some refried beans (if using).

NOTAS

✻ *If you're not used to spicy food, use only 1 serrano pepper. If serrano peppers are unavailable, use 1 jalapeño pepper. To add a smoky twist, use 2 chipotle peppers in adobo sauce (from a can) instead of the serrano peppers.*

✻ *To make green chilaquiles, simply substitute tomatillos for the plum tomatoes in the salsa recipe, then follow the rest of the steps as is.*

✻ *You can prepare chilaquiles ahead by making the salsa and frying the tortilla chips—but storing separately. Cook the chips in the sauce just before serving.*

MIGAS

Migas is a delightfully simple Mexican breakfast dish that is loved by many, both young and old. Like Chilaquiles (page 34), migas are an excellent way to use leftover corn tortillas. Many people prepare migas by simply mixing the crispy tortillas with eggs, and that's enough to make a delicious breakfast, but others also add tomato, onion, and peppers like in this recipe. Migas, like many other Mexican breakfasts, are traditionally served with beans from the pot or refried topped with crumbled queso fresco. People usually serve this dish with a spicy salsa and some sliced avocado on the side.

PREP TIME: 10 minutes	**COOK TIME:** 15 minutes	**YIELD:** 2 servings

4 corn tortillas (preferably day-old; see Notas)

¼ cup (60 ml) vegetable oil

⅓ cup (40 g) chopped white onion

1 serrano pepper or ½ jalapeño pepper, finely chopped

1 cup (180 g) chopped plum tomato (about 2 large tomatoes)

4 large eggs

Salt

FOR SERVING

Crumbled queso fresco

Black beans (from the pot or refried)

Sliced avocado (optional)

Thinly sliced green onion (optional)

NOTAS

* Day-old tortillas will make the crispiest tortilla chips.

* Add the tortilla chips before the eggs are completely cooked, or you risk overcooking the eggs.

1. Using a knife or a pair of kitchen scissors, cut the corn tortillas into 1½-inch (4 cm) squares.

2. In a large skillet, heat the oil over medium-high heat. Once hot, place the tortilla squares in the oil and stir and turn the pieces as needed until they acquire a medium golden-brown color, about 6 minutes. (Make sure to use a frying pan that is large enough, so you do not overcrowd the pan.) Remove the pan from the heat and transfer the fried tortilla pieces to a paper towel–lined plate to drain any excess oil.

3. Return the skillet to the stove and turn the heat to medium-high. Add the white onion and cook and stir for a few seconds, then stir in the pepper. Keep cooking for about 2 minutes. Add the tomato and cook for about 3 minutes more. Crack the eggs into the pan, but do not stir. Once the egg whites are cooked around the edges, gently stir the eggs. Once the egg yolks start to cook (see Notas), stir in the tortilla chips, season with salt, and gently mix them together with the eggs. When the eggs are cooked to your liking, remove the pan from the heat.

4. Serve immediately (to preserve their crispiness) with crumbled cheese, black beans, and slices of avocado and green onion (if using).

QUESADILLA DE JAMÓN

Ham and Cheese Quesadilla

The humble *quesadilla de jamón* is an unmistakable classic, and every schoolchild in Mexico has probably eaten it at least once in their life. Besides being popular for breakfast, this dish can also serve as a packed lunch, a midday nibble, a light dinner, or even a midnight snack. The type of quesadilla in this recipe is called a *sincronizada*, and what distinguishes it from a regular quesadilla is that it's not folded in half but made by layering two tortillas on top of each other, with the cheese and filling in between.

PREP TIME: 5 minutes	**COOK TIME:** 10 minutes	**YIELD:** 1 serving

1 teaspoon vegetable oil or butter (optional; see Notas)

2 medium-size flour tortillas

2 ounces (57 g) Oaxaca, Muenster, or Monterey Jack cheese, shredded or sliced

2 ounces (57 g) cooked ham (about 2 slices)

1. Heat a comal over medium-high heat and add the oil (if using), using a paper towel to spread the oil all over the pan.

2. When the pan is hot, place one of the tortillas on it. Layer on half the cheese, both ham slices, and then the rest of the cheese. Cover with the remaining tortilla and, using a cast-iron press or spatula, press down on the quesadilla. Once the cheese starts to melt, use a spatula to check the underside of the tortilla for any golden-brown spots. The cooking time will depend on the type of pan you have as well as the cheese you are using.

3. Once the underside has golden-brown spots, carefully flip the quesadilla over and keep cooking until both sides are golden brown and the cheese is melted. For a really crispy texture, reduce the heat and let it cook for a few more minutes.

4. Transfer to a cutting board, cut into wedges, and serve.

NOTAS

✖ *The vegetable oil or butter is optional if you are using a nonstick pan, but I like using it because it helps to give the tortillas a crispy surface.*

✖ *You can use other types of fillings, such as shredded chicken, sliced mushrooms, refried beans, cooked ground beef, leftover grilled meats, vegetables, and so on, and serve with guacamole, salsa, and/or Mexican crema.*

✖ *If you are making several quesadillas, preheat the oven to 300°F (150°C) and place them on a baking sheet to keep warm while you finish cooking the rest.*

MOLLETES

Molletes are often served for breakfast, both at home and in restaurants. They are popular with students from elementary school to college and are excellent when you have a busy day ahead but only a few minutes to prepare breakfast. Besides their simplicity, one thing that makes molletes great are how forgiving they are. You can make them with almost any bread you have on hand and use any cheese that melts. Molletes are also customizable and can be as simple or extravagant as you like. Although the traditional mollete is only topped with refried beans, melted cheese, and pico de gallo (like in this recipe), there are many people who like to add ham or Chorizo (page 122) as an extra topping.

PREP TIME: 5 minutes	**COOK TIME:** 10 minutes	**YIELD:** 2 servings

PICO DE GALLO (SEE NOTAS)

½ cup (90 g) chopped tomato

¼ cup (35 g) finely chopped white onion

1 small serrano pepper, finely chopped, or 1 tablespoon finely chopped jalapeño pepper

¼ cup (10 g) chopped fresh cilantro

Salt

MOLLETES

2 Bolillos (page 215) or 2 lengths (6 inches/15 cm each) crusty French bread

2 tablespoons butter, softened

½ cup (120 g) refried black beans, warmed

¾ cup (85 g) shredded queso Oaxaca (or a melting cheese, such as mozzarella, Muenster, or Monterey Jack)

1 link Mexican chorizo, casing removed, crumbled, and cooked (optional)

1. To make the pico de gallo: In a medium bowl, gently mix the tomato, onion, pepper, and cilantro until well combined. Season with salt.

2. To make the molletes: Preheat the oven to 400°F (205°C). Cut the bread in half lengthwise and remove some of the inside crumb. Spread the butter on the insides of the bread pieces and place them, insides facing up, on a baking sheet. Bake for 4 to 5 minutes, until lightly golden and crispy. Keep the oven on. (You can also toast the bread directly on a comal over medium heat.)

3. Remove the bread from the baking sheet and spread the refried beans on each piece. Top with the cheese, followed by the cooked chorizo (if using). Place back onto the baking sheet and into the oven and continue baking until the cheese has melted, about 5 minutes.

4. Serve with the pico de gallo.

NOTAS

* *Some people add a few drops of lime juice to the pico de gallo; however, it makes the pico de gallo a bit watery. You can also use other salsas, such as a roasted salsa.*

* *In Mexico, you can also find sweet molletes prepared only with the buttered bread and topped with sugar.*

PAPAS A LA MEXICANA

Mexican-Style Potatoes

When a dish is prepared *a la Mexicana*, it means that it includes tomato, onion, and jalapeño (or serrano) peppers, and *papas a la Mexicana* is no exception. This is a dish that is more commonly prepared at home than in restaurants, and it is enjoyed for breakfast, lunch, or dinner. It is a comforting meal that is both vegetarian and budget-friendly. Besides serving it by itself, you can also top this dish with a fried egg, or use it as a filling for tacos, burritos, and gorditas. It can also be used as a side dish.

PREP TIME: 10 minutes	**COOK TIME:** 20 minutes	**YIELD:** 2 servings

2 tablespoons vegetable oil

2 cups (280 g) peeled and diced potatoes (see Notas)

⅓ cup (35 g) diced white onion

1 serrano or jalapeño pepper (see Notas), finely chopped

2 Roma tomatoes, diced (about 1¼ cups/225 g)

Salt

FOR SERVING (OPTIONAL)

Warm corn tortillas

Fried eggs

1. In a large skillet, heat the oil over medium heat. Add the diced potatoes and cook for 8 to 10 minutes, stirring frequently to avoid burning them and making sure all sides of the potatoes are golden brown.

2. Add the onion and cook and stir until translucent, about 3 minutes. Add the pepper and cook for 2 more minutes, stirring occasionally.

3. Check the potatoes for doneness, then add the chopped tomatoes, season with salt, and gently stir them in with the potatoes, onion, and pepper. Cook for 2 to 3 minutes. (I like the tomato cubes to still have some shape when serving, so this step is a quick one, but you can cook a little longer if you like.)

4. Serve by itself with tortillas (or as tacos) or with a side of fried eggs.

NOTAS

* *Although white potatoes are commonly used in Mexico, you can also make this dish with Idaho or russet potatoes.*

* *You can add another pepper for more heat.*

* *This dish can be garnished with a little chopped fresh cilantro and crumbled queso fresco.*

PAPAS CON CHORIZO

Chorizo with Potatoes

A hearty combination, *papas con chorizo* (also called *chorizo con papas*) is one of the most beloved ways to eat chorizo in the morning, alongside Huevos con Chorizo (page 27). This dish can be served with a side of beans or topped with eggs, but it can also be used as a filling for breakfast tacos, burritos, sopes, gorditas, and more. You can also make tortas with it, which is something I used to do when I was a schoolgirl. Usually when making this, the potatoes are fried slowly along with the chorizo, which takes a long time; my version achieves the same results but cuts down on the cooking time by boiling the potatoes first.

PREP TIME: 5 minutes	**COOK TIME:** 20 minutes	**YIELD:** 4 servings

1½ pounds (680 g) white or red potatoes, peeled and cut into ½-inch (13 mm) cubes

2 tablespoons vegetable oil, plus more if needed

10 ounces (283 g) Mexican chorizo, casings removed

⅓ cup (40 g) finely chopped white onion

Salt

FOR SERVING (OPTIONAL)

Beans of choice

Warm corn or flour tortillas

Spicy salsa of choice

1. Place the potatoes in a medium saucepan, cover with water, and cook over medium-high heat. Once the water comes to a boil, reduce the heat to medium-low and cook for 8 to 10 minutes. (The potatoes do not need to be thoroughly cooked, just tender; they will finish cooking in the skillet with the chorizo.) Drain the potatoes.

2. While the potatoes are cooking, heat the oil in a large skillet over medium-high heat. Crumble the chorizo, add it to the pan, and cook for about 8 minutes, or until cooked through, stirring often to make sure it does not stick to the pan. Stir in the cooked potatoes and the onion, combining well to allow the chorizo flavor to coat the potatoes. Add more oil if needed to finish cooking the potatoes to your liking and keep them from sticking to the pan. (Some people like their potatoes crispy, while others let them cook longer until they are a little soft.) Season with salt.

3. Serve on a plate with a side of beans, or in tortillas as tacos topped with salsa.

NOTA *If you want to cook the chorizo and potatoes together in the same pan (without boiling the potatoes first), start cooking the chorizo as indicated in step 2. Once the chorizo is cooked, remove it from the pan and transfer to a plate. Add the raw potatoes and onion to the pan and cook over low heat, stirring occasionally, until the potatoes are cooked, about 15 minutes. Then stir in the cooked chorizo to reheat.*

SALCHICHAS A LA MEXICANA

Although it might be surprising for some to hear, hot dog sausages are a common ingredient in Mexican home cooking. They are easily added to beans, soups, and stews and can also be scrambled with eggs for a quick breakfast. They are also used as a filling for some tortas. The availability and affordability of hot dog sausages makes them an excellent ingredient to plan an inexpensive meal around, and this recipe is a great example of that. *Salchichas a la Mexicana*, like all other dishes with *a la Mexicana* in their name, uses tomato, onion, and pepper. Here, these ingredients are used to make a lightly spicy sauce, which is combined with the sliced sausages for a simple yet filling meal. This dish is mostly made at home and not easily found in restaurants and is often served with a side of refried beans and tortillas. My family loves this dish, especially served with some bolillos to soak up all that delicious sauce.

PREP TIME: 10 minutes	COOK TIME: 20 minutes	YIELD: 2 servings

1 tablespoon vegetable or olive oil

¼ cup (35 g) chopped white onion

1 serrano or jalapeño pepper, finely chopped (see Notas)

1 small clove garlic, finely chopped

4 hot dog sausages, cut into bite-size slices (see Notas)

1¼ cups (225 g) chopped plum tomato (about 2½ tomatoes)

Salt

FOR SERVING

Refried beans (black or pinto)

Warm Bolillos (page 215) or corn tortillas

1. In a medium skillet, heat the oil over medium heat. Add the onion and cook and stir until translucent, 2 to 3 minutes. Add the pepper and garlic and cook and stir for about 2 minutes. Add the hot dogs and cook, stirring occasionally, for 4 minutes, or until the edges start to turn a light-golden color.

2. Add the tomatoes and cook for about 5 minutes, or until they start to simmer. Season with salt, cover the pan with the lid, and reduce the heat to low. Cook for another 5 to 7 minutes, until the tomatoes are cooked and have released all their juices.

3. Serve with beans and bolillos or tortillas.

NOTAS

✖ *If you don't like spicy food, only add half of the pepper.*

✖ *I use standard 6-inch (15 cm) hot dog sausages, but you can use other types of sausages too.*

✖ *Some people like to add chopped fresh cilantro to this dish. If you want to, add 2 tablespoons near the end of the cooking time.*

✖ *You can also use this dish as a filling for tacos or tortas.*

CHILORIO

Chilorio is a flavorful pork stew from the northern state of Sinaloa, where it can be found being sold by vendors at the local markets, as well as being made at home. This dish is similar to other stews around Mexico called "pork adobo," but chilorio is slightly drier and almost always served shredded (usually with a side of beans). Chilorio is also more commonly eaten for breakfast than at other meals. This dish can be used as a filling for tacos, burritos, gorditas, sopes, and more. Besides being quite versatile, it also stores well, making it a convenient dish to keep in the fridge or freezer.

PREP TIME: 20 minutes	**COOK TIME:** 1 hour	**YIELD:** 6 servings

2 pounds (907 g) pork butt or shoulder, cut into 3-inch (7.5-cm) cubes

1 bay leaf

1 teaspoon salt, plus more to taste

4 ancho peppers, seeds and veins removed

2 guajillo peppers, seeds and veins removed

6 tablespoons lard

¼ cup (60 ml) apple cider or white vinegar

1 teaspoon dried Mexican oregano

½ teaspoon ground cumin

¼ teaspoon black pepper, plus more to taste

6 coriander seeds

4 cloves garlic

FOR SERVING

Warm flour tortillas

Hot sauce of choice

1. Add the meat, 1½ cups (360 ml) of water, the bay leaf, and the salt to a large saucepan. Cover and bring to a boil over medium-high heat. Once boiling, reduce the heat to low and simmer for 45 to 60 minutes, until the meat is fork-tender. Remove the lid and keep cooking, letting the water evaporate.

2. Add the lard to the pan with the meat. Increase the heat to medium-high and let the meat slightly brown all over. Turn the heat off, then remove and reserve the bay leaf. Shred the meat using two forks, then return it to the same pan.

3. While the meat cooks, place the ancho and guajillo peppers in a medium saucepan with 2 cups (480 ml) of water. Cover with the lid and cook over medium-low heat for 15 minutes, or until the peppers look soft. Let cool for at least 5 minutes, reserving the cooking water.

4. Place the cooked peppers, 1 cup (240 ml) of the reserved cooking water, and the vinegar in a blender. Add the reserved bay leaf, oregano, cumin, black pepper, coriander seeds, and garlic and process until a smooth sauce.

5. Pour the sauce over the shredded meat in the pan using a fine-mesh strainer. Turn the heat to medium-high and cook for 5 minutes, stirring occasionally. Reduce the heat to a simmer and season with salt and black pepper. Let simmer for 10 to 15 minutes, until the sauce has reduced, turned a darker color, and fat starts to float to the surface.

6. Serve with tortillas and hot sauce (since this is not a spicy dish).

NOTAS

- *Do not worry if the chilorio starts to look a little dry; this stew is supposed to be on the drier side.*
- *As with any recipe, some home cooks use their own combination of dried peppers to make this dish. Such a mix could include two or more of these varieties: pasilla, Colorado, guajillo, and ancho.*
- *You can also add 2 whole cloves and a 1-inch (2.5-cm) piece of a cinnamon stick to the blender while making the sauce.*
- *Chilorio keeps well in the freezer for up to 4 months when stored properly.*

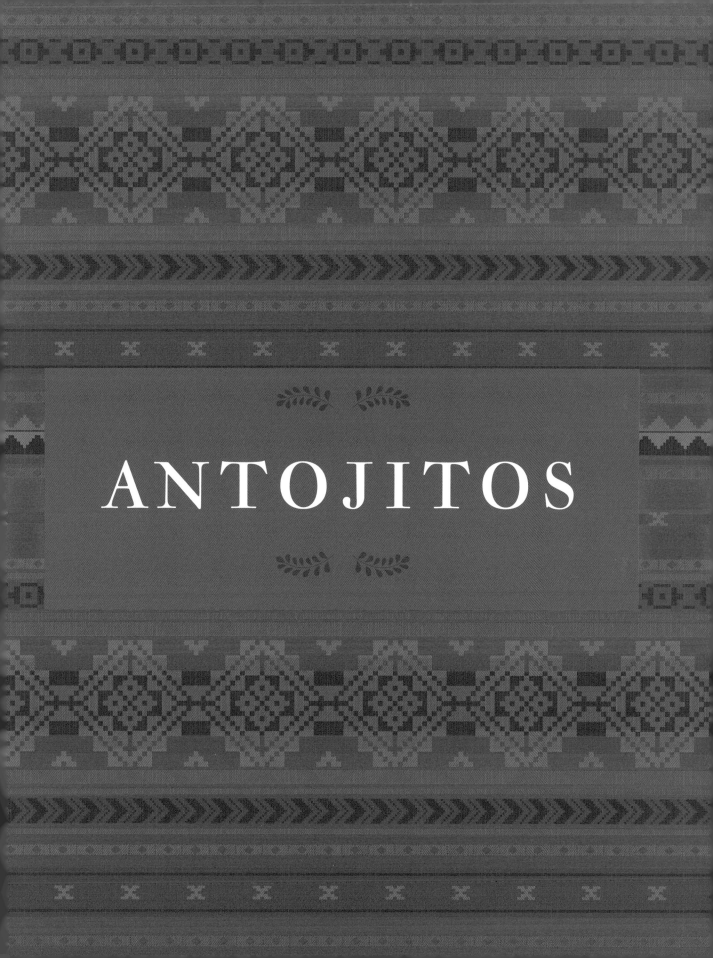

ANTOJITOS

GORDITAS

Gorditas are similar to tortillas but thicker and smaller. Their added thickness allows them to be opened to make a pocket that is stuffed with savory fillings. A favorite hand-held meal, gorditas can be found for sale in Mexico in restaurants and at fairs, markets, and street-food stands. The beauty of a gordita is that it is a vessel you can fill with anything you want, be it a stew, refried beans, or leftovers you have in the fridge. You can even make a cheese gordita by simply stuffing it with a slice of queso fresco. Alternatively, you can whip up some scrambled eggs to make gorditas for breakfast.

PREP TIME: 15 minutes	**COOK TIME:** 25 minutes	**YIELD:** 9 gorditas

GORDITAS

1½ cups (150 g) masa harina for tortillas

½ teaspoon salt

FILLING

1 cup (200 to 240 g) refried beans, Picadillo Sencillo (page 89), or filling of choice (see Notas)

FOR SERVING

1½ cups (85 g) shredded lettuce

¼ white onion, thinly sliced

1 tomato, thinly sliced

1 cup (120 g) crumbled queso fresco

Salsa of choice

1. To make the gorditas: In a medium bowl, combine the masa harina and salt. Slowly add 1¼ cups (300 ml) of water and knead to form a uniform mixture. If the dough feels dry, add more water, a spoonful at a time, until the dough is soft and manageable. The texture needs to feel like play dough to work; it does not need to be sticky. (Depending on the humidity where you live, you will need to add about 2 more tablespoons of water to the dough, and you should also keep a small bowl of water nearby to moisten the dough as needed. This dough tends to get dry, so cover it with a moist kitchen or paper towel while you continue working.)

2. Divide the dough into 9 equal-size balls. You can place them back in the bowl or on your kitchen counter but cover them with a moistened kitchen or paper towel. Heat a comal over medium-high heat. The surface needs to be hot when you place the gorditas on it to keep them from sticking.

3. To form the gorditas, place a dough ball between two 7 x 7-inch (18 x 18 cm) plastic sheets cut from a freezer bag. Using a tortilla press or a heavy glass pie dish, press down on the ball to form a gordita that is no more than ¼ inch (6 mm) thick and 4 inches (20 cm) in diameter (see Notas). Open the tortilla press and remove the top plastic sheet. Pick up the gordita, holding it with the bottom plastic sheet. Gently flip it onto the palm of your other hand so that the bottom plastic sheet is now on top. Remove the plastic sheet, then place the gordita on the hot comal to cook.

(continued)

4. Let the gordita cook for about 2 minutes, or until it starts forming light-brown spots on the bottom side, then flip and cook for another 2 minutes. Once it has formed spots on the other side, flip again, and cook for an additional 20 seconds. After the second flip, it should inflate (or "puff up") slightly, for a total cooking time of around 4½ minutes. Remove it from the comal and cover with a clean cloth napkin or kitchen towel to keep warm. As soon as you can handle the gordita, use a paring knife to make an incision around the edge—cut around about one-third of its circumference—creating an opening just big enough to add the filling. Return the gordita to the napkin to keep it warm while you finish preparing and cooking the remaining dough balls. You can press them in the tortilla press while you have a gordita cooking; just keep a watchful eye on it.

5. Once you've finished making all the gorditas, add the filling of your choice. Serve hot with the lettuce, onion, tomato, cheese, and salsa(s).

NOTAS

✖ *Forming gorditas in a tortilla press is the same process as making tortillas, but don't press down as far. If using a glass baking dish, gently press on the ball of dough, making sure to use even pressure. The benefit of using a glass baking dish is that you can see through it, allowing you to observe how the gordita is being formed as you press down on it.*

✖ *You can use any type of filling you have on hand. The filling needs to be warm and ready to use when the gorditas come off the comal. Other types of fillings include plain shredded cheese, cooked potatoes, chorizo, chicharrones, carnitas, and leftovers.*

SOPES

Sopes are like thick tortillas that have a hand-formed border around them, which makes the sope an excellent vessel for a variety of toppings, including shredded chicken, beef, or pork, as well as stews, such as Picadillo Sencillo (page 89), chicharrón en salsa verde, or tinga de pollo. Sopes often have some refried beans spread on the bottom and are garnished with tomato, onion, shredded lettuce, crumbled cheese, crema, and salsa. Sopes are eaten by hand and can be enjoyed for breakfast, lunch, and dinner. Like a true antojito, sopes can be found at street stands throughout most Mexican cities, as well as in restaurants, diners, and homes. The size, thickness, and shape of the sopes can vary from cook to cook and from town to town, as can the garnishes. You can also find them topped with shredded cabbage, avocado, radish slices, and even pickled carrots.

PREP TIME: 30 minutes	**COOK TIME:** 20 minutes	**YIELD:** 10 sopes

SOPES

1½ cups (150 g) masa harina for tortillas

1¼ cups (300 ml) warm water, plus more if needed

¼ cup vegetable oil (60 ml) or lard (50 g)

TOPPINGS

1 cup (240 g) refried beans (black or pinto)

1½ cups cooked shredded beef (330 g) or chicken (300 g)

FOR GARNISHING AND SERVING

2 cups (110 g) finely shredded lettuce

¼ cup (35 g) finely chopped white onion

½ cup (90 g) sliced or diced tomatoes

1 avocado, sliced

½ cup (60 g) crumbled queso fresco (see Notas on page 56)

½ cup (120 ml) Mexican crema (see Notas on page 56)

Spicy salsa of choice

⅓ cup (40 g) thinly sliced radish (optional)

Pickled Jalapeño Peppers and Carrots (page 184) (optional)

1. To make the sopes, in a medium bowl, combine the masa harina and warm water and knead until you have a uniform texture. If the dough feels dry, add more water, a spoonful at a time, until the dough is soft and manageable, like play dough; it does not need to be sticky. (If you live in a humid place, the dough will not need too much water; otherwise, make sure that the dough has enough moisture to avoid any cracking on the surface of the sopes.)

2. Cover the dough with a wet kitchen or paper towel to help keep the dough moist. (Always keep a small bowl of water next to your work area to keep your hands and the dough moist.) Divide the dough into 10 equal-size balls and cover them with the kitchen towel. Heat a comal over medium-high heat. The surface needs to be hot when you place the sopes on it to keep them from sticking.

3. To form the sopes, place a slightly flattened dough ball between two 7 x 7-inch (18 x 18 cm) plastic sheets cut from a freezer bag. Using a tortilla press or a heavy glass pie dish, gently press down on the dough to form a tortilla shape that is ¼ inch (6 mm) thick and 4½ inches (11.5 cm) in diameter. Open the tortilla press and remove the top square of plastic. Pick up the tortilla, holding it with the bottom square of plastic. Gently flip it onto the palm of your other hand so that the bottom plastic sheet is now on top. Remove the plastic sheet, then place the tortilla on the hot comal, in a fast but gentle move, to cook.

(continued)

4. Cook the tortilla for 1 minute, then flip it over (do not let it cook longer or the dough will dry and crack). Flip it again after another minute; this last cooking period takes only 20 to 30 seconds, until it puffs up (if it does not puff up, you can press it gently to force it to). Remove from the comal with the help of a spatula. Cover the tortilla with a dry kitchen towel, let cool for 30 to 45 seconds, then form the border by placing the tortilla on a flat surface and using your thumb and index finger to pinch the dough around its perimeter, creating a wall that is perpendicular to the flat center of the sope. You must do this quickly while the dough is still hot, because if you let the tortilla cool, it will no longer be possible to shape it into a sope. Cover again with the kitchen towel while you finish preparing and cooking the remaining dough balls.

5. In a large skillet or comal, heat the oil over medium-high heat. Working in batches, place the sopes in the skillet and lightly cook on both sides, about 30 seconds per side, or until they turn a slight golden color. Transfer to a paper towel–lined plate to absorb any excess oil.

6. To assemble the sopes, spread refried beans on the inner surface of the sopes, then top with shredded beef or chicken, and garnish with shredded lettuce, onion, tomato, avocado, cheese, and crema. Serve with salsa, sliced radish (if using), and pickled jalapeños and carrots (if using).

NOTAS

* *You can substitute the queso fresco with panela, Cotija, feta, or Parmesan cheese.*

* *Making sopes requires a certain amount of time and preparation, which is why it's better to make them when you have some leftovers in your fridge, such as refried beans and beef or chicken from a stew. This way you don't have to spend time preparing a stew or other filling from scratch.*

TACOS AL PASTOR

Tacos al pastor, also known as *tacos de trompo* or *tacos de adobada*, are classic street tacos that are popular throughout Mexico, as well as in many taco restaurants in the United States. To make these tacos, thin slices of pork are marinated in a flavorful adobo sauce and then stacked on a large skewer in an inverted cone shape and cooked on a vertical spit. This cooking process is similar to how shawarma is made in many Middle Eastern cuisines. Traditionally, the cooked al pastor meat is shaved from the cone before being served in warm corn tortillas, but you can also cook the meat on your stovetop or grill at home.

PREP TIME: 30 minutes plus 4 hours marinating time	**COOK TIME:** 30 minutes	**YIELD:** 8 or 12 tacos

ADOBO MARINADE AND FILLING

4 guajillo peppers, seeds and veins removed

1 ounce (28 g) achiote (annatto) paste

¼ cup (60 ml) pineapple juice (you can use the juice from canned pineapple slices; see Tacos below)

¼ cup (60 ml) white vinegar

3 cloves garlic

1 teaspoon dried Mexican oregano

½ teaspoon ground cumin

¼ teaspoon black pepper, plus more to taste

2 whole cloves

1¼ teaspoons salt, plus more to taste

2 pounds (907 g) pork butt or shoulder, cut into ⅓-inch-thick (8.5 mm) steaks

TACOS

2 tablespoons vegetable oil, plus more if needed

1 medium white onion, thinly sliced

1 can (8 ounces/227 g) pineapple slices or 3 slices fresh pineapple

8 medium-size or 12 street taco–size corn tortillas

1. To make the adobo marinade and filling: Place the guajillo peppers in a medium saucepan and completely cover with water. Let simmer over medium heat for about 15 minutes, or until they become soft. Let cool, then drain and remove the peppers from the saucepan.

2. Add the softened guajillo peppers to a blender along with the achiote paste, pineapple juice, white vinegar, garlic, oregano, cumin, black pepper, cloves, and salt. Process until a very smooth sauce. Pour the sauce slowly through a fine-mesh strainer into a large bowl to get a homogenous texture. Taste the sauce and adjust the salt if needed.

3. Season the pork steaks with salt and pepper, then place them in the bowl with the adobo sauce, evenly coating the meat with your hands or a pastry brush. Let marinate, covered, in the refrigerator for at least 4 hours, or preferably overnight.

4. To make the tacos: In a large skillet, heat the vegetable oil over medium-high heat. Add the marinated pork and onion slices, making sure not to overcrowd the pan, and cook for 12 to 15 minutes, turning the steaks as needed to keep them from sticking. Transfer the pork steaks to a cutting board and chop them into small pieces.

5. Return the chopped meat to the skillet over medium-high heat, stirring the pieces and making sure all edges get browned, 3 to 4 minutes. (If needed, add an extra drizzle of oil to the skillet.) Toward the end of this step, cut the pineapple slices into small pieces and add them to the skillet to warm them a bit (keep them separate from the meat).

FOR GARNISHING AND SERVING

½ cup (20 g) finely chopped fresh cilantro

½ cup (65 g) finely chopped onion

Spicy salsa of choice (see Notas)

Lime wedges

6. Warm the tortillas on a hot comal. Assemble the tacos by placing some of the al pastor meat and cooked onions onto each warm tortilla. Top the tacos with the chopped cilantro and onion and pineapple pieces. Serve with salsa and lime wedges for squeezing.

NOTAS

- *Salsa verde is the most popular type of salsa used to top these tacos, but you can use any salsa that you like.*
- *Grilling the pork will give the meat a smoky flavor. You can also grill the pineapple slices before cutting them.*
- *Making extra al pastor meat is always a good idea; you can use it later to make more tacos or al pastor quesadillas* (gringas).

TACOS DE ALAMBRE

These tacos are prepared with steak, bacon, onion, and peppers, which is the same combination of ingredients that is used to make grilled skewers (kebabs). In Mexico, these skewers are called *alambres*, which is how this dish got the name *tacos de alambre*. Instead of cooking the ingredients on a skewer on the grill, these tacos are prepared by frying everything in a skillet, making for an easier preparation. You can substitute the steak with chicken, shrimp, or even mushrooms.

PREP TIME: 10 minutes	**COOK TIME:** 20 minutes	**YIELD:** 8 or 12 tacos

1½ pounds (680 g) top sirloin steak, cut into ½-inch (13 mm) cubes

Salt and black pepper

Juice of ½ lime

6 ounces (170 g) bacon, cut into ½-inch (13 mm) pieces

1 cup (110 g) chopped white onion (about ½ medium onion)

1½ cups (220 g) chopped red and green bell pepper

6 ounces (170 g) queso Oaxaca, shredded, or sliced Muenster cheese (see Notas)

12 corn tortillas or
8 medium-size flour tortillas

FOR SERVING

Salsa of choice

1. Place the steak cubes in a medium bowl, season with salt and black pepper, add the lime juice, and mix well.

2. Heat a large skillet over medium-high heat. Once the skillet is hot, add the bacon and cook for about 4 minutes, or until it starts to release fat and the edges turn light brown. Transfer the bacon to a paper towel–lined plate. (At this point, you can remove some of the fat from the skillet, but you want to keep some for the next step.)

3. Add the steak to the skillet with the bacon fat and cook over medium-high heat for about 6 minutes, or until the meat starts to brown. Stir in the onion and bell pepper and continue cooking for 3 to 4 minutes. Add the cooked bacon back into the pan and stir.

4. Scatter the cheese all over the meat and vegetables. Wait until it starts melting, then remove the skillet from the heat and cover with the lid. Let the cheese melt a little bit longer while you warm the tortillas on a hot comal.

5. Assemble the tacos as soon as the tortillas are warmed and serve with salsa.

NOTAS

✶ *You can use any type of melting cheese, such as Monterey Jack or mozzarella, although Muenster is my first choice if queso Oaxaca isn't available.*

✶ *If making these tacos with shrimp or chicken, season them with 1 tablespoon of soy sauce in addition to the lime juice in step 1.*

BAJA-STYLE FISH TACOS

This recipe always reminds me of the first time I visited Baja California, in the early '90s. One day during our trip, my husband invited me to have some tacos for lunch at a taco stand, and I was surprised that they only served fish tacos. Despite growing up in a town on the Gulf of Mexico, I had never seen fish tacos before! After trying them, I was intrigued as to why we didn't make them on the eastern coast of Mexico. Nowadays, you can find them in restaurants throughout Mexico and the United States. I prepare all the toppings before making the batter and frying the fish, because you need to assemble the tacos immediately once the fish is cooked.

PREP TIME: 25 minutes	**COOK TIME:** 20 minutes	**YIELD:** 8 tacos

PICO DE GALLO

2 plum tomatoes, diced

½ cup (55 g) chopped white onion

2 serrano peppers, chopped

⅓ cup (15 g) finely chopped fresh cilantro

Juice of 1 lime

½ teaspoon salt

CREAMY DRESSING

1 chipotle pepper in adobo sauce (from the can)

⅓ cup (80 ml) Mexican crema or sour cream (see Notas)

⅓ cup (80 ml) mayonnaise

1 tablespoon fresh lime juice

Salt and black pepper

BATTER

1 cup (130 g) all-purpose flour

½ teaspoon dried Mexican oregano

½ teaspoon salt

½ teaspoon black pepper

⅓ teaspoon garlic powder

1 bottle or can light beer (see Notas), at room temperature

1. To make the pico de gallo: Place the tomatoes, onion, serrano peppers, and cilantro in a medium bowl, then add the lime juice. Add the salt and stir well.

2. To make the creamy dressing: Add the chipotle pepper to a blender along with the crema, mayonnaise, and the 1 tablespoon lime juice and process until smooth and creamy. Season with salt and black pepper and stir.

3. To make the batter: Place the 1 cup (130 g) flour in a medium bowl, then crush the oregano with your fingers and add it to the flour along with the ½ teaspoon each salt and black pepper and the garlic powder. Mix well. Gently pour a small amount of the beer into the flour while mixing everything with a whisk. (You will NOT need to use the whole bottle/can; just enough to make a batter that has a texture similar to pancake batter.)

4. To make the tacos: In a large skillet, heat the oil over medium-high heat. While the oil heats up, cut the fish, against the grain, into strips about 4 inches (10 cm) long. Season with salt and black pepper. Place the ½ cup (65 g) flour on a plate, then proceed to dredge the fish strips in the flour, making sure that they are well coated.

5. Once the oil is hot, dip the floured strips of fish into the batter, coating them completely, then place them into the oil, working in batches as not to overcrowd the pan. Cook until they are golden brown and crispy, flipping to cook all over, 5 to 6 minutes total. Transfer to a paper towel–lined plate to absorb any excess oil.

TACOS

1½ cups (360 ml) vegetable oil

1 pound (454 g) cod, halibut, tilapia, or red snapper fillets

Salt and black pepper

½ cup (65 g) all-purpose flour

8 corn tortillas

FOR GARNISHING AND SERVING

1½ cups (140 g) finely shredded cabbage

Lime wedges

Spicy salsa of choice

6. Warm the tortillas on a hot comal. To assemble the tacos, place 1 or 2 pieces of fish on each tortilla, top with the shredded cabbage and pico de gallo, and drizzle with the creamy dressing. Serve with lime wedges for squeezing and salsa.

NOTAS

✱ *You can add diced pineapple or mango to the pico de gallo, which will complement these tacos well.*

✱ *To make the creamy dressing spicier, add more chipotle peppers. If you don't want it to be spicy, add only a few drops of adobo sauce from the canned chipotles. You also can make the creamy dressing with only the mayonnaise.*

✱ *You can add ¼ teaspoon of paprika to the batter to give it more flavor. You can substitute the beer with sparkling mineral water or plain water mixed with 1 teaspoon of baking powder. This batter can also be used with shrimp.*

TACOS DE SUADERO

When I think about the tacos in Mexico City, *tacos de suadero* always come to mind. These are some of the most iconic tacos found there, and their popularity has spread to many parts of the country. The cut of beef, *suadero*, is called "rose meat" in the United States. It has a light pink color, hence the name, and while its tougher texture takes a little more time to cook, the end result is juicy and very tasty.

PREP TIME: 20 minutes	**COOK TIME:** 2 hours (see Notas)	**YIELD:** 12 tacos

2 pounds (907 g) suadero beef (see Notas and photo below)

Salt

2 tablespoons lard or vegetable oil

12 corn tortillas

FOR GARNISHING AND SERVING

½ cup (65 g) finely chopped white onion

½ cup (20 g) finely chopped fresh cilantro

Spicy salsa of choice

Thinly sliced radish (optional)

Grilled spring onions (see Nota on page 81 for grilling instructions) (optional)

Grilled serrano peppers (see page 232 for roasting instructions) (optional)

Lime wedges

1. Season the meat with salt. Heat the lard in a medium pot over medium-high heat. Add the meat and sear each side for about 1 minute per side.

2. Cover the meat with 4 cups (1 quart/950 ml) of water (or enough to cover the meat) and cook for about 2 hours over medium heat, or until the meat is tender (see Notas). Add more water if needed during this process, in case the meat is not tender yet.

3. Once the meat is tender and the water has reduced completely, remove the meat and finely chop it on a cutting board. Return it to the pot to lightly brown in the leftover grease.

4. Warm the corn tortillas on a hot comal preheated over medium heat.

5. Assemble the tacos by placing some chopped suadero onto the warm tortillas. Top with the chopped onion and cilantro and season with salt and serve with the salsa, sliced radish (if using), grilled onions and peppers (if using), and lime wedges for squeezing.

NOTAS

✳ *The suadero cannot be replaced with another cut of beef or meat. In the US, suadero can be found in Latin markets and butcher shops. In Latin America, suadero is also known as matambre and sobrebarriga.*

✳ *Suadero is a tough meat that needs some time to cook until tender. If you have a pressure cooker or Instant Pot, the meat will only take about 50 minutes on the "Manual" setting on high pressure to become tender. You can also cook it in a slow cooker for 6 hours on the low setting.*

✳ *Sometimes I cook the meat in advance and just brown it on the comal (while warming the tortillas) when I'm ready to make the tacos.*

TACOS DORADOS DE PAPA

Crispy Potato Tacos

These tacos are loved by everyone regardless of age, but they're especially a hit with children. They're great for parties, family gatherings, and everyday dinners. Along with Tortitas de Papa (page 147), they are particularly popular during Lent, when many families opt for meatless meals. This recipe is surprisingly convenient because it uses very few ingredients, and the tacos can even be made ahead of time. I like serving them with shredded cabbage, crumbled cheese, and pico de gallo.

PREP TIME: 25 minutes	**COOK TIME:** 35 minutes	**YIELD:** 12 tacos

PICO DE GALLO

1 cup (180 g) diced tomato

½ cup (55 g) chopped white onion

2 serrano peppers, chopped

½ cup (20 g) finely chopped fresh cilantro

1 tablespoon fresh lime juice

Salt

TACOS

3 medium potatoes of choice (about 18 ounces/510 g), skins on and left whole (see Notas)

Salt and black pepper

½ cup (120 ml) vegetable oil, plus more if needed

12 corn tortillas

FOR GARNISHING AND SERVING

2 cups finely shredded cabbage (190 g) or lettuce (110 g)

⅓ cup (40 g) crumbled queso Cotija or fresco

1 avocado, sliced (optional)

½ cup (120 ml) Mexican crema (optional)

1. To make the pico de gallo: Place the tomato, onion, serrano peppers, and cilantro in a medium bowl, then add the lime juice. Season with salt and stir well.

2. To make the tacos: Place the potatoes in a medium saucepan and cover with cold water. Place the pot over medium-high heat, bring to a boil, and cook until the potatoes are fork-tender, about 20 minutes. Drain the potatoes and transfer to a bowl. Let cool, then remove their skins. Season with salt and black pepper, then mash the potatoes until a smooth, paste-like consistency.

3. In a large skillet, heat the oil over medium-high heat. Meanwhile, gently warm the tortillas, one at a time, on a hot comal to make them more pliable. Cover with a cloth napkin or kitchen towel to keep warm.

4. To assemble the tacos, place 2 tablespoons of the mashed potatoes on one-half of a warmed tortilla. Fold the tortilla in half and secure each side with a toothpick. Repeat with the remaining filling and tortillas.

5. Place the tacos in the hot oil, working in batches if necessary, and cook for about 1 minute and 30 seconds per side, or until the tacos are crispy and golden brown. Transfer to a paper towel–lined plate to absorb any excess oil.

6. Remove the toothpicks from the tacos, then garnish with the shredded cabbage, crumbled cheese, pico de gallo, avocado slices (if using) and crema (if using).

NOTAS

✖ *Do not peel or cut the potatoes before cooking them, as this will make them absorb more water, which can cause the oil to splatter during the frying process.*

✖ *You can substitute the cheese with Parmesan or feta.*

✖ *If you don't have toothpicks, press down on the tacos with a wooden spatula against the bottom of the skillet when frying to keep them closed until they harden.*

✖ *If you make these tacos ahead of time, reheat them in an oven preheated to 350°F (175°C) for 5 to 6 minutes.*

SOUPS

SOPA DE FRIJOL CON CHORIZO

Black Bean Soup with Chorizo

There are many varieties of bean soups found throughout Mexico, and this one in particular is inspired by a dish I had many years ago in the town of Poza Rica in Veracruz. It's made using black beans, tomato, and chorizo, making for a rich flavor combination. You can top it with avocado, cilantro, and thin tortilla chips. It's a delicious and hearty meal that's perfect for warming you up during the colder months.

PREP TIME: 10 minutes	**COOK TIME:** 30 minutes	**YIELD:** 4 servings

6 ounces (180 g) Mexican chorizo (about 2 medium-size chorizo links), casings removed

½ cup (65 g) chopped white onion

1 poblano pepper, seeds and veins removed and finely chopped (optional)

2 serrano peppers or 1 jalapeño pepper, finely chopped

2 cups (360 g) diced tomatoes

4 cups (700 g) cooked black beans, plus 1½ cups (360 ml) bean broth (see Notas)

FOR GARNISHING

¼ cup (60 ml) vegetable oil

4 corn tortillas, cut into thin strips

¼ cup (10 g) chopped fresh cilantro

Sliced avocado

1. Heat a large saucepan over medium-high heat. Crumble the chorizo, add it to the pan, and cook it in its own fat until cooked through, about 8 minutes. (If the chorizo does not render enough fat, add 1 tablespoon of vegetable oil to the pan.)

2. Add the onion and cook and stir until it starts turning translucent, 2 to 3 minutes. Stir in the peppers and cook for 3 more minutes. Add the tomatoes and cook, stirring occasionally, for 6 to 8 minutes.

3. Add the cooked beans, the bean broth, and 1 cup (240 ml) of water and cook until the soup comes to a boil, then reduce the heat and let gently simmer for 8 to 10 minutes.

4. While the soup is cooking, in a large skillet, heat the oil over medium-high heat. Add the tortilla strips and fry until light golden and crispy, about 8 minutes. Transfer to a paper towel–lined plate to absorb any excess oil.

5. Serve the soup in bowls and garnish with the fried tortilla strips, chopped cilantro, and avocado slices.

NOTAS

✱ *If using canned black beans, use 2 cans (15 ounces/425 g each) and the liquid from the cans for the broth.*

✱ *This soup is perfect for freezing, making it a convenient option for those days when you want to take a break from cooking. Just prepare a big batch and store it in individual portions in freezer bags or freezer-safe airtight containers.*

SOPA DE PAPA

Mexican Potato Soup

Delicious and soul-warming, this soup is simple to make and only requires a few ingredients. You can serve it as the first course for a comforting winter lunch, or enjoy it by itself as a light dinner. Both adults and children love this soup, and it is easily adapted to make it vegan (see Notas) so that everyone can enjoy it.

PREP TIME: 15 minutes	**COOK TIME:** 20 minutes	**YIELD:** 4 servings

3 Roma tomatoes (about 13 ounces/ 369 g)

4 medium golden potatoes (about 1¼ pounds/567 g), peeled

1 large clove garlic

5 cups (1.2 L) chicken broth (see Notas), divided

1 tablespoon vegetable or olive oil

¼ medium white onion, finely chopped

Salt and black pepper

FOR GARNISHING AND SERVING

Chopped fresh parsley

Warm corn tortillas or crusty bread (such as Bolillos on page 215)

NOTAS

✳ *Use vegetable broth to make this soup vegan.*

✳ *For herb lovers, add ½ teaspoon of dried Mexican oregano or a couple of fresh epazote leaves to the broth in step 5, 5 minutes before it's finished cooking.*

✳ *To make this soup more robust, serve with diced queso panela or fresco for topping.*

1. Heat a comal over medium-high heat. Once hot, place the tomatoes on the comal and roast them, turning them every few minutes to achieve an even roasting, about 10 minutes. (They will not be completely cooked through, but this step will give them a nice roasted flavor.)

2. While the tomatoes are roasting, cut the potatoes into sticks that are 2 inches (5 cm) long and about ⅜ inch (1 cm) thick (don't worry about being exact with the dimensions).

3. Transfer the roasted tomatoes to a blender along with the garlic and 1½ cups (360 ml) of the broth. Process until a smooth sauce.

4. In a large saucepan, heat the oil over medium heat. Add the onion and cook and stir until it starts turning translucent, 2 to 3 minutes.

5. Pour the sauce from the blender into the saucepan through a fine-mesh strainer. Bring the sauce to a boil over medium-high heat, then add the potatoes and the remaining 3½ cups (840 ml) broth. Taste and season with salt and pepper. Keep cooking until the tomato broth comes to a boil, then reduce the heat and cover the saucepan with the lid, leaving some space to allow the pot to release steam. Continue cooking for about 15 minutes. Check the potatoes for doneness, making sure you do not overcook them, as the potatoes will keep cooking with the heat of the broth. (The type of potatoes you use and the size you cut them will affect the cooking time.)

6. Ladle the soup into medium bowls, garnish with parsley, and serve with warm tortillas or bread.

CALDO DE CAMARÓN

Shrimp Soup

This is one of the most common soups served at seafood restaurants in Mexico. Although it's eaten year-round, it is especially popular around Easter. Because caldo de camarón is prevalent across the country, there are bound to be many variations. For example, my mom likes to dilute a little bit of corn masa with water and add it to the soup, giving it a slightly thicker texture.

PREP TIME: 15 minutes	**COOK TIME:** 30 minutes	**YIELD:** 4 servings

SHRIMP BROTH

Shells from 1 pound (454 g) raw shrimp (see Soup below)

¼ medium white onion

2 cloves garlic

1 bay leaf

SOUP

1 pound (454 g) plum tomatoes (about 4 tomatoes)

¼ medium white onion

2 cloves garlic, unpeeled

1 chipotle pepper in adobo sauce (from the can) (optional)

2 tablespoons olive oil

1¼ cups (175 g) peeled and medium diced carrots

1¼ cups (175 g) peeled and medium diced potatoes

1 pound (454 g) raw shrimp, shells removed and deveined (reserve shells to make the broth)

4 large fresh epazote leaves (see Notas)

Salt and black pepper

FOR SERVING

Warm corn tortillas

Lime wedges

1. To make the shrimp broth: Place the shrimp shells, onion, garlic, and bay leaf in a medium saucepan along with 5 cups (1.2 L) of water and turn the heat to medium-high. Once boiling, reduce the heat to low and let simmer for 6 to 8 minutes. Remove from the heat.

2. To make the soup: While the broth is simmering, place a comal over medium-high heat. Once hot, place the tomatoes, onion, and garlic on the comal and roast them, turning occasionally, for about 8 minutes. Remove the garlic from the comal after about 2 minutes because it takes less time to roast (if you leave it too long, it will burn and have a bitter taste). Transfer the roasted tomatoes, onion, and garlic (peeled first) to a blender along with the chipotle pepper (if using). Process until you have a fine texture. If needed, chop the tomatoes before placing them in the blender.

3. In a medium pot, heat the oil over medium heat. Add the carrots and cook for 2 minutes. Add the potatoes and cook for 6 to 7 minutes, stirring often to keep them from sticking. Pour the tomato sauce into the pot through a fine-mesh strainer. Bring to a boil over medium-high heat, then reduce the heat to low and let simmer for 10 minutes.

4. Add the shrimp broth to the pot through the fine-mesh strainer, then stir in the shrimp. Keep simmering until the shrimp are a light-orange color but look firm, 5 to 7 minutes (total time will depend on the size of the shrimp). (Do not overcook them, or they will have a rubbery texture.) Add the epazote to the pot and cook for 2 more minutes. Season with salt and pepper.

5. Immediately ladle the soup into bowls and serve with warm tortillas and lime wedges for squeezing.

NOTAS

✳ *You can add more chipotle peppers in adobo sauce to add heat.*

✳ *If you can only find dried epazote, use 1 teaspoon. You can also skip it or use ½ teaspoon of dried Mexican oregano in its place.*

✳ *Not everyone roasts the tomatoes, onion, and garlic, but it gives an added richness to the flavor of the soup.*

SOPA DE HONGOS

Mushroom Soup

In the small towns of central Mexico, you can find several types of mushrooms growing during the rainy season. They are usually sold at local municipal markets by people who come from the small farms in the countryside. In Mexico, we enjoy these mushrooms in stews, soups, and other dishes, and this simple but nourishing soup is just one example of that. It's perfect for a cold, rainy day when you want something warming yet not too filling.

PREP TIME: 5 minutes	**COOK TIME:** 20 minutes	**YIELD:** 4 servings

1 tablespoon vegetable or olive oil

1 tablespoon butter

½ cup (65 g) finely chopped white onion

2 cloves garlic, minced

2 guajillo peppers, seeds and veins removed and cut into rings

1 pound (454 g) white mushrooms (see Notas), stems removed and sliced

6 cups (1½ quarts/1.4 L) chicken broth

4 fresh epazote leaves (or 1 teaspoon dried epazote)

Salt and black pepper

FOR SERVING

Warm corn tortillas or crusty bread (such as Boilillos on page 215)

1. In a medium pot, heat the oil and butter over medium heat (see Notas). Add the onion, garlic, and guajillo pepper rings and cook and stir until the onion is soft, about 2 minutes.

2. Add the mushrooms, stir, and then cover the pot. Let simmer over medium-low heat until the mushrooms are soft and have released some of their juices, 4 to 5 minutes.

3. Stir in the broth and epazote leaves. When the soup starts simmering, season with salt and pepper.

4. Keep simmering over low heat for about 10 minutes to let the flavors blend.

5. Ladle the soup into bowls and serve with warm tortillas or bread.

NOTAS

✳ *You can use either the oil or the butter to cook the vegetables. I add the butter because it gives a rich flavor to the soup.*

✳ *Cremini and portobello mushrooms are also good options for this soup.*

✳ *You can also add squash blossoms near the end of the cooking process. You can find them at farmers' markets when in season. You can also add 1 cup (145 g) of fresh corn kernels (or a 15-ounce/425-g can of drained corn) to make this dish a little more filling. Add it in step 2 along with the mushrooms.*

✳ *To make a vegan version, omit the butter and use vegetable broth.*

CALDO TLALPEÑO

Caldo Tlalpeño is a popular soup that can be found in restaurants throughout Mexico, from small eateries to large chains. Its name indicates that this soup is from a place called Tlalpan, but there are several regions that claim to be the place where it originated, as well as several stories explaining how it came to be. Though this soup is often served as the starter course at a restaurant, a big, hearty bowl is enough to be a complete meal. You can find some easy recipes with only chicken, chickpeas, and carrots, and complex ones with squash, potatoes, rice, and more. One of the things that makes caldo Tlalpeño so special and easily recognizable is that it's usually topped with diced avocado, crumbled cheese, and a chipotle pepper in adobo sauce in the center and served with tostadas on the side or tortilla strips on top.

PREP TIME: 10 minutes	**COOK TIME:** 1 hour and 10 minutes	**YIELD:** 4 servings

CHICKEN AND BROTH

20 ounces (567 g) bone-in, skinless chicken breast

¼ medium white onion

1 large clove garlic

1 teaspoon salt

SOUP

2 tablespoons vegetable oil

9 ounces (255 g) carrots, peeled and diced (about 2 large carrots)

10 ounces (283 g) chopped tomatoes (about 2 large tomatoes)

1 clove garlic

2 tablespoons finely chopped white onion

3½ ounces (100 g) green beans, chopped

1 cup (160 g) cooked chickpeas (see Notas)

2 sprigs fresh cilantro

4 fresh epazote leaves (or 1 teaspoon dried epazote)

Salt

1. To make the chicken and broth: Place the chicken in a large stockpot along with the onion quarter and garlic clove, cover with 8 cups (2 quarts/1.9 L) of water, and add the salt. Cover the pot with the lid, place over high heat, and bring to a boil. Once boiling, reduce the heat to low and let simmer for about 45 minutes, or until the chicken is tender and easy to shred.

2. Strain the chicken broth and set aside to cool. When cool enough to handle, shred the chicken meat and discard the bones.

3. To make the soup: Using the same pot, heat the oil over medium heat. Add the carrots and cook, stirring occasionally, for about 5 minutes.

4. While the carrots are cooking, place the tomatoes and garlic clove in a blender along with 1 cup (240 ml) of the reserved chicken broth. Process until a smooth sauce.

5. Add the chopped onion to the pot with the carrots and cook until translucent, about 3 minutes. Pour the tomato sauce into the pot and cook for 8 more minutes.

6. Add the remaining reserved chicken broth, green beans, chickpeas, cilantro, epazote, and shredded chicken to the pot. Let gently simmer for 6 minutes. Season with salt.

FOR GARNISHING AND SERVING

1 avocado, diced

4 ounces (113 g) queso fresco or panela, diced

4 chipotle peppers in adobo sauce (from the can)

Warm corn tortillas or tostadas

Lime wedges (optional)

7. Ladle the soup, including the shredded chicken, vegetables, and broth, into bowls. Serve with avocado, cheese, and chipotle peppers on small plates for garnishing and enjoy with tortillas or tostadas and lime wedges for squeezing (if using).

. . . .

NOTAS

✖ *You can also add 2 sprigs of parsley and 1 celery rib to give more flavor to the chicken broth.*

✖ *You can use a can (15.5 to 16 ounces/439 to 454 g) of drained and rinsed chickpeas.*

CARNE EN SU JUGO

Carne en su jugo literally translates to "meat in its juices." This recipe comes from Guadalajara in the state of Jalisco and consists of chopped beef that is cooked in its juices along with a tomatillo sauce. The tartness of the tomatillo helps to compensate for all that meaty flavor, creating a delicious and balanced mouthful.

PREP TIME: 10 minutes	**COOK TIME:** 36 minutes	**YIELD:** 6 servings

1 tablespoon soy sauce

1 tablespoon fresh lime juice

Salt and black pepper

1½ pounds (680 g) top round sirloin (or any other lean cut of beef), cut into thin, bite-size pieces

4 tomatillos

2 serrano peppers

8 ounces (227 g) bacon, diced

2 cloves garlic, chopped

¼ cup (30 g) chopped white onion

¼ cup (10 g) chopped fresh cilantro

4 cups (1 quart/950 ml) chicken broth (see Notas), divided

2 cups (350 g) cooked pinto beans, warmed

FOR GARNISHING AND SERVING

3 tablespoons finely chopped white onion

6 tablespoons finely chopped fresh cilantro

⅓ cup (40 g) thinly sliced radish

6 grilled spring onions (see Notas)

Sliced avocado

Tortilla chips

1 lime, cut into wedges

1. In a large bowl, mix the soy sauce, lime juice, and black pepper until well combined. Add the beef pieces to the bowl and let marinate.

2. Meanwhile, place the tomatillos and serrano peppers in a medium saucepan and cover with water. Bring to a boil over medium-high heat, then reduce the heat to low and let simmer for 10 to 12 minutes, until they are soft.

3. Place a medium Dutch oven over medium heat. Add the bacon and cook until crisp, about 8 minutes. Transfer the bacon to a paper towel–lined plate to absorb any excess grease. Remove the excess bacon fat, leaving about 1 tablespoon in the pot. Add the marinated meat and its liquid to the pot and cook over medium heat for about 8 minutes, stirring occasionally; the meat will start releasing some of its juices.

4. While the meat cooks, place the cooked tomatillos and serrano peppers in a blender with the garlic, onion, cilantro, and 1 cup (240 ml) of the broth. Process until smooth. Pour this mixture over the meat and add the remaining 3 cups (360 ml) broth. Taste and season with salt and pepper. Bring to a boil over medium-high heat, then reduce the heat to low, cover, and let simmer for about 20 minutes, or until the meat is tender.

5. Divide the pinto beans among six bowls, then add the meat on top along with its broth. Serve the bacon, white onion, cilantro, radish, spring onions, avocado, tortilla chips, and lime wedges on small plates for garnishing.

NOTA *To grill the spring onions, heat 1 tablespoon of oil in a large skillet over medium-high heat. Add the onions and cook, turning occasionally, for even cooking, 8 to 10 minutes.*

SOPA DE MILPA

Sopa de milpa is a traditional dish from the central states of Mexico, and its name roughly translates to "cornfield soup." It derives its name from the farming system called *milpa*, in which corn, beans, and peppers are planted together on the same piece of land. It is a sustainable farming practice that has been used since pre-Hispanic times. The milpas can also include squash, tomatoes, and tomatillos, all ingredients that are consumed in rural communities. This is a beautifully simple soup that showcases the bounty of the Mexican countryside.

PREP TIME: 10 minutes	**COOK TIME:** 20 minutes	**YIELD:** 6 servings

2½ cups (365 g) fresh corn kernels (about 2 large ears of corn)

2 fresh epazote leaves (see Notas)

2 tablespoons butter

½ cup (65 g) finely chopped white onion

2 small cloves garlic, minced

2½ cups (290 g) diced squash or zucchini (about 2 medium squash)

2 poblano peppers (see Notas), roasted, seeds and veins removed, and cut into strips or diced (see page 232 for roasting instructions)

12 squash blossoms, cleaned and stems removed

6 cups (1½ quarts/1.4 L) chicken broth

Salt and black pepper

FOR GARNISHING AND SERVING

1½ cups (180 g) crumbled queso panela or fresco

Warm corn tortillas

1. In a medium saucepan, combine the corn, 2 cups (480 ml) of water, and the epazote leaves. Bring to a simmer over medium heat and cook for about 5 minutes.

2. Meanwhile, in a medium pot, melt the butter over medium-low heat. Add the onion and cook for 2 minutes, then add the garlic and cook for 1 more minute, or until fragrant. Add the squash and cook for 5 minutes until slightly softened.

3. Add the cooked corn kernels and their cooking liquid to the pot and stir to combine well. Increase the heat to medium-high and add the poblano peppers and squash blossoms. Stir well. Add the chicken broth and let simmer for an additional 5 to 7 minutes, until all the vegetables are tender and cooked. Taste the soup and season with salt and black pepper.

4. Ladle the soup into bowls, garnish with the cheese, and serve with warm tortillas.

NOTAS

* This soup is prepared very quickly, so it's important to have all the ingredients prepped before you start cooking.

* If you can only find dried epazote, use ½ teaspoon. You can also substitute ¼ teaspoon of dried Mexican oregano for epazote in the final cooking step.

* Other vegetables you can add to this soup are chayotes and green beans.

SOPA DE CONCHITAS CON VERDURAS

Pasta Shell Soup with Vegetables

Sopa de conchitas is a popular soup in Mexican homes and small diners. The basic version only has pasta shells in a tomato-based broth, but some people also like to add vegetables to it, like in this recipe. These tasty pasta soups are usually eaten for lunch or are served as a dinner starter, although the soup is enjoyed as a main meal by some people. For many, pasta soups are a comfort food, and this one is no exception.

PREP TIME: 5 minutes	**COOK TIME:** 25 minutes	**YIELD:** 4 servings

1 tablespoon vegetable oil

¾ cup (105 g) peeled and diced carrot

1 large tomato or 2 plum tomatoes, chopped (about 10 ounces/283 g)

¼ cup (35 g) chopped white onion

1 clove garlic, chopped

1 cup (112 g) shell (concha) pasta (see Notas)

4 cups (1 quart/950 ml) chicken broth

Salt

1½ cups (50 g) baby spinach

NOTAS

✴ *This soup can be made with other pasta shapes, such as macaroni or farfalle.*

✴ *Feel free to add any vegetables you like or skip them entirely.*

✴ *This soup keeps well in the refrigerator for up to 3 days or you can freeze for up to 3 weeks.*

1. In a medium saucepan, heat the vegetable oil over medium-high heat. Add the carrot and cook, stirring occasionally, for about 5 minutes, or until semi-cooked and bright orange.

2. While the carrots are cooking, place the tomatoes, onion, and garlic in a blender along with 2 cups (480 ml) of water and process until a smooth sauce.

3. Add the shell pasta to the saucepan with the carrots and cook, stirring constantly, for about 3 minutes, or until the pasta obtains a light-golden color. (It is okay if the pasta has some golden-brown spots, as they add more flavor.)

4. Pour the tomato sauce and broth into the saucepan and stir. Season with salt. Increase the heat to high and bring the soup to a quick boil. Once boiling, reduce the heat to low, cover with the lid, and cook for 10 more minutes.

5. Add the spinach, stir, and cook for 5 more minutes. Immediately remove the saucepan from the heat to avoid overcooking the spinach.

6. Serve the soup in small bowls.

MAIN DISHES

PICADILLO SENCILLO

Basic Picadillo

As the name suggests, this *picadillo* is a basic version of the traditional one found in Mexico (and many other Latin American countries). The more elaborate version of picadillo can have ingredients such as carrots, peas, and even olives and raisins, depending on the region. This simple picadillo is also based on ground beef in a tomato sauce, but it only has diced potatoes added, which is why it is often referred to as *carne molida con papas* (ground beef with potatoes). *Picadillo sencillo* is a classic comfort food, and it's a dish that you can rely on when you're not feeling in the mood to make anything complicated but still want something tasty and filling. Besides serving it on a plate with rice and beans, you can also use it as a filling for tacos, sopes, gorditas, empanadas, tamales, and more.

PREP TIME: 15 minutes	**COOK TIME:** 25 minutes	**YIELD:** 6 servings

2 tablespoons vegetable oil

1 pound (454 g) ground beef (see Nota)

⅓ cup (35 g) diced white onion

2 cloves garlic, finely chopped

1 serrano or jalapeño pepper, finely chopped

1½ cups (210 g) diced potato

1 pound (454 g) plum tomatoes (3 or 4 tomatoes), diced

1 teaspoon beef or chicken bouillon granules

Salt and black pepper

⅓ cup (15 g) finely chopped fresh cilantro

FOR SERVING

White or red rice

Black or pinto beans (from the pot or refried)

Warm corn tortillas

1. In a large skillet, heat the oil over medium-high heat. Add the ground beef and cook, using a wooden spoon to break it up into smaller pieces, until it turns brown, about 8 minutes.

2. Add the onion and garlic to the skillet and cook and stir until the onion turns translucent, 2 to 3 minutes. Add the serrano pepper and the diced potato, stir well, and continue cooking for about 5 minutes, or until the potatoes are slightly tender but still firm.

3. Add the diced tomatoes and bouillon to the skillet and stir well. (As the tomatoes release their juices, the bouillon will dissolve, enriching the flavors of the picadillo.) Cover with the lid, then reduce the heat and let simmer until the potatoes are completely cooked and the tomatoes have formed a thick sauce, 10 to 12 minutes. Season the picadillo with salt and pepper and stir in the cilantro.

4. Serve with rice, beans, and warm tortillas.

NOTA *I usually use ground beef that is 85% lean/15% fat, which renders some fat while it is cooking, but you can easily remove any excess fat with a spoon. If you want to cook this recipe with a leaner meat, such as ground turkey or ground chicken, it may require additional oil in the skillet during the cooking process.*

BEEF SHANK STEW

This stew is one of my husband's favorites. He's a big fan of dishes that incorporate tomatoes, olives, raisins, and capers, so this recipe is a real winner. The beef is first cooked slowly until it's tender, and then it's combined with a thick, rich tomato sauce, making for a truly delicious and satisfying meal. It's ideal for when you're having people over for Sunday supper. This dish also works well for a celebration or other special occasion.

PREP TIME: 15 minutes	**COOK TIME:** 1 hour and 40 minutes (see Notas)	**YIELD:** 8 servings

BEEF

4 pounds (1.8 kg) beef shank

½ medium onion

4 cloves garlic

1 bay leaf

STEW

2 tablespoons olive or vegetable oil

¾ cup (85 g) diced white onion

2 large cloves garlic, minced

2 cans (28 ounces/794 g each) whole peeled tomatoes

3 large carrots, peeled and sliced into ⅓-inch-thick (8.5 mm) rounds

3 medium white potatoes, peeled and cubed

½ cup (120 ml) dry white wine (see Notas)

½ cup (75 g) raisins

⅓ cup (40 g) sliced pimiento-stuffed Spanish olives

1 tablespoon capers, drained

1 teaspoon dried Mexican oregano

1 bay leaf

2 teaspoons fresh thyme or 1 teaspoon dried thyme

Salt and black pepper

1. To make the beef: Place the beef shank in a large pot with the onion half, garlic cloves, and bay leaf. Cover with about 8 cups (2 quarts/1.9 L) of water and cook, covered, over medium heat until fork-tender, about 1½ hours. Add warm water as needed while cooking.

2. Meanwhile, make the stew: In a large pot or Dutch oven, heat the oil over medium heat. Add the diced onion and cook and stir until translucent, 2 to 3 minutes. Add the minced garlic and cook and stir for 1 more minute.

3. Add the canned tomatoes and their juices to the pot and bring to a boil over medium-high heat, then reduce the heat to low and let simmer for about 15 minutes, or until the tomatoes start to lose their shape. Use a potato masher to mash the tomatoes into a chunky texture, like a chunky salsa.

4. Add the carrots and cook for 5 minutes, then stir in the potatoes and cook for 8 minutes more.

5. Add the cooked meat, white wine, raisins, olives, capers, oregano, bay leaf, and thyme. Stir well to blend all the flavors. Season with salt and black pepper. Keep cooking over low heat for 8 to 10 minutes, until the vegetables are tender but still hold their shape. (If the sauce gets too dry and the meat is not fork-tender, add ½ cup/120 ml of the meat cooking broth to continue cooking the stew.) Remove and discard the bay leaf.

6. Garnish with the fresh parsley and serve with warm, crusty bread or white rice and pickled jalapeño peppers and carrots (if using).

FOR GARNISHING AND SERVING

¼ cup (13 g) finely chopped fresh parsley

Warm crusty bread (such as Bolillos on page 215) or white rice

Pickled Jalapeño Peppers and Carrots (page 184) (optional)

NOTAS

- *You can cook the meat in an Instant Pot in 40 minutes on the "Manual" setting on high pressure, or 50 minutes if using a stovetop pressure cooker once the valve starts releasing steam. You can also cook the meat in a slow cooker for 6 hours on the low setting.*
- *If you don't have white wine on hand, you can use 2 tablespoons of white vinegar mixed with 6 tablespoons of water.*

SALPICÓN DE RES

Shredded Beef Salad

The name *salpicón* usually refers to a fresh salad-like dish made with a shredded or minced meat as its base. Throughout Latin America, several countries have their version of salpicón made with chicken, seafood, or beef. In Mexico, the most popular version is beef salpicón, although you can also find some versions made with deer or rabbit meat (we also have seafood salpicón). *Salpicón de res* is an excellent dish to enjoy on hot summer days and is great for entertaining. You can cook the meat one or two days ahead, store it in the fridge, and then mix it with the rest of the ingredients at serving time. Salpicón is usually served with tostadas and some pickled jalapeño peppers. If you are invited to a summer picnic or potluck, this dish is a good option to bring along; just make sure to add the dressing right before serving to keep the lettuce from wilting.

PREP TIME: 20 minutes	**COOK TIME:** 2 hours and 30 minutes (see Notas)	**YIELD:** 6 servings

BEEF

1½ pounds (680 g) skirt steak or eye round roast, cut into 2½- to 3-inch (6 to 7.5 cm) cubes

½ medium white onion

2 cloves garlic

1 bay leaf

Salt and black pepper

DRESSING

¼ cup (60 ml) vegetable or olive oil

1 tablespoon white or sherry vinegar (see Notas)

½ teaspoon dried Mexican oregano

Salt and black pepper

SALAD

3 cups (165 g) finely shredded romaine lettuce

¼ medium white onion, sliced into rings

4 radishes, thinly sliced

1. To make the beef: Place the meat, onion half, garlic cloves, and bay leaf in a medium stockpot. Cover with water and the lid and bring to a boil over a medium-high heat. Once boiling, reduce the heat and let simmer until the meat is tender and can be easily shredded with a fork, about 2½ hours.

2. Meanwhile, make the dressing: In a small bowl, mix the oil and vinegar until emulsified. Crush the oregano with your fingers and add it to the dressing. Season with salt and black pepper.

3. Transfer the cooked meat to a large bowl to cool for about 20 minutes. Once cool enough to handle, finely shred the beef using two forks and season with salt and black pepper.

4. To assemble the salad: Place the shredded beef in a large serving bowl and gently toss with the lettuce, sliced onion, radishes, tomato, and olives.

5. Garnish with the avocado slices, drizzle with the dressing, and serve with the corn tostadas and pickled jalapeños and carrots.

1 large tomato, diced

6 pimiento-stuffed Spanish olives, sliced

FOR SERVING

1 avocado, sliced

12 corn tostadas

Pickled Jalapeño Peppers and Carrots (page 184)

NOTAS

❌ *You can cook the meat in an Instant Pot or a pressure cooker for 45 minutes on the "Manual" setting on high pressure. You can also cook it in a slow cooker for about 6 hours on the high setting.*

❌ *Traditionally, white vinegar is used for the dressing, but I prefer the flavor of sherry vinegar in this salad.*

❌ *I like to serve this salad with small cups of the beef broth that the meat was cooked in as a side dish. To try this, after removing the cooked meat from the broth, add a small sprig of thyme to the broth and let simmer for 15 minutes. Serve the broth garnished with chopped cilantro, onion, and serrano pepper.*

BIRRIA DE RES

Beef Birria

Birria is a soup that hails from the state of Jalisco, along Mexico's western coast. It is traditionally made with goat, lamb, or sheep meat, or a combination of several types of meat. The adobo sauce is made using a blend of spices and dried peppers. Cooked birria meat has become a popular taco filling in the United States, but in Mexico, it is still enjoyed in a bowl with the tasty broth. Using a combination of meats is common in restaurants or local birria eateries known as *birrierias*. This recipe uses beef because it is more accessible and popular, but you can also use beef ribs or cuts of meat meant for pot roast. Just make sure that you add a cut of meat with some bone in it because it adds lots of flavor to the birria.

PREP TIME: 20 minutes plus 4 hours marinating time	**COOK TIME:** 4 hours (see Notas on page 96)	**YIELD:** 6 servings

2 pounds (907 g) chuck roast

2 pounds (907 g) beef shank (see Notas on page 96)

Salt and black pepper

3 ancho peppers, seeds and veins removed

6 guajillo peppers, seeds and veins removed

½ medium white onion, thickly sliced

6 large cloves garlic, unpeeled

2 large tomatoes

4 whole cloves

½ teaspoon cumin seeds

½ teaspoon black peppercorns

1 teaspoon dried Mexican oregano

½ teaspoon dried marjoram

1 Mexican cinnamon stick (1 inch/ 2.5 cm long)

½ cup (120 ml) white vinegar

1. Season the meat with salt and black pepper, then place it in a large baking dish (about 13 inches/33 cm long).

2. Slightly toast the ancho and guajillo peppers on a comal over medium heat, making sure not to burn them (burnt peppers make the dish taste bitter). Transfer the peppers to a medium bowl filled with hot water and let soak for 20 minutes.

3. Meanwhile, on the same comal, over low heat, toast the onion slices, garlic cloves, and tomatoes until they turn golden, rotating them for even toasting, about 3 minutes for the onion and garlic and 8 minutes for the tomatoes. Peel the garlic cloves and transfer all the ingredients to a blender. Toast the whole cloves, cumin seeds, and peppercorns for a few seconds, then transfer to the blender. Add the oregano, marjoram, cinnamon stick, and vinegar to the blender.

4. Once the peppers are soft, drain, and add them to the blender. Process with the rest of the ingredients until a smooth sauce. (If your blender is having a hard time processing, add a few tablespoons of water.) Season the sauce with salt.

5. Pour the sauce over the meat, making sure it is completely covered. Cover the baking dish with aluminum foil and refrigerate overnight or for at least 4 hours to allow all the meat to absorb the flavors (see Notas on page 96).

(continued)

FOR GARNISHING AND SERVING

⅓ cup (25 g) finely chopped fresh cilantro

⅔ cup (85 g) finely chopped white onion

2 teaspoons dried Mexican oregano (optional)

Warm corn tortillas

Spicy salsa of choice

Lime wedges (optional)

6. Preheat the oven to 350°F (175°F). Bake the meat for about 4 hours, or until it is fork-tender.

7. Ladle the warm birria with its broth into bowls, garnish with chopped cilantro and onion and oregano (if using) and serve with tortillas, salsa, and lime wedges for squeezing (if using).

NOTAS

✶ *You can make this dish in an Instant Pot or a pressure cooker on the "Manual" setting on high pressure for approximately 1 hour. If the meat is easy to shred, then it's ready to serve; if the meat is still a little hard to shred, cook for another 10 to 15 minutes. You can also cook this dish in a slow cooker for 6 to 8 hours on the low setting.*

✶ *Depending on the sizes of the bones in the beef shank, this recipe will render 6 to 8 portions. Instead of beef shank, you can buy only a large piece (4 pounds/ 1.8 kg) of chuck roast plus some bones (like the ones sold for soup). You can also make your own combination of cuts of meat.*

✶ *The birria in this recipe more closely resembles a stew than a soup. If you want it to have more broth, add 4 to 6 cups (1 to 1½ quarts/0.9 to 1.4 L) of water to the baking dish before baking. The broth will come out very flavorful. If you only want the birria meat for tacos, then adding water is not necessary; the meat and sauce will suffice.*

✶ *Some cooks like to add a ¼-inch (6 mm) piece of ginger to the sauce. Simply add it to the blender with the spices in step 3.*

✶ *Use leftover birria to make birria quesadillas.*

ENMOLADAS

Chicken Mole Enchiladas

Similar to enchiladas, *enmoladas* are rolled corn tortillas stuffed with shredded chicken and smothered with a delicious sauce—in this case, *mole*. Enmoladas is the perfect dish to make when you have some leftover mole poblano sauce, but if you don't have any, you can still make them using mole paste (see Notas on page 99). You can stuff these enmoladas with shredded chicken, or use crumbled queso fresco for a vegetarian version. They are usually served with a drizzle of crema and some crumbled cheese on top. This dish can be enjoyed by itself or with a lettuce salad.

PREP TIME: 20 minutes	**COOK TIME:** 15 minutes	**YIELD:** 12 enmoladas

3 cups (720 ml) mole sauce

Chicken broth (optional)

¼ cup (60 ml) vegetable oil

12 corn tortillas

2½ cups (375 g) cooked shredded chicken (see Notas on page 99), warmed

1 cup (120 g) crumbled queso fresco (see Notas on page 99)

FOR GARNISHING

¾ cup (180 g) Mexicana crema

Finely shredded lettuce (optional)

Crumbled queso fresco

⅓ medium red onion, thinly sliced

1. Warm the mole sauce in a large skillet over medium-low heat. The consistency of the mole should be similar to a light gravy; if you think it's too thick, add some chicken broth.

2. In a separate large skillet, heat the vegetable oil over medium-high heat. Once the oil is hot, reduce the heat to medium and, using kitchen tongs, quickly fry each tortilla, one at a time, on each side for a few seconds. You do not want the tortillas to be crispy, so only cook them long enough to still be pliable (this step is done very quickly). Drain each tortilla using a slotted spoon and transfer to a paper towel–lined plate. Cover the fried tortillas with aluminum foil to keep them warm.

3. Using the kitchen tongs, dip each tortilla into the warm mole sauce, making sure that each tortilla is completely submerged, then transfer to a plate for assembling. (This step is also done quickly to avoid breaking the tortillas.)

4. Add the filling (shredded chicken or crumbled cheese) down the center of the tortilla, then roll or fold it closed and transfer to a serving plate with the help of a spatula (see Notas on page 99). Repeat with the remaining tortillas and filling. If needed, spoon more mole sauce over the enmoladas.

5. Right before serving, garnish with a drizzle of crema and top with lettuce (if using), some more crumbled queso fresco, and onion slices.

(continued)

NOTAS

✻ *Mole sauce and mole paste are available online or at Latin grocery stores. You only need to dilute the mole paste to get it to a creamy consistency (similar to a light gravy), then you're all set to make enmoladas. The mole sauce should have a smooth consistency and not be too thick. If you find that it is too thick, thin it with chicken broth or water; if it is too watery, gently boil it to thicken and reduce it. If you are using store-bought mole paste, you can prepare it by following the instructions on the packaging or you can enhance it by following the instructions on page 181 to make it more flavorful.*

✻ *Chicken broth is generally used to dilute mole sauce and mole paste, but you can also use water. Keep in mind that if you use water, it will dilute the flavor of the mole.*

✻ *You can use leftover rotisserie chicken for this recipe.*

✻ *You can also use queso panela or farmer, feta, or Parmesan cheese.*

✻ *I like to use a separate plate for assembling the enmoladas before placing them on the serving dish and garnishing them.*

ARROZ CON POLLO

Many Latin-American countries have their own version of this dish, with some adding ingredients such as olives, green peppers, and other vegetables depending on the region. Even within Mexico, the ingredients can vary from household to household. My mom, for example, would add slices of hot dog sausages, as an economical way to extend the dish for our large family. The beauty of *arroz con pollo* is that it's an easy one-pan meal (although you can also make it in a pot).

PREP TIME: 15 minutes plus 15 minutes soaking time	**COOK TIME:** 35 minutes	**YIELD:** 4 servings

1 cup (185 g) long-grain white rice

4 bone-in, skin-on chicken thighs (see Notas)

Salt and black pepper

2 tablespoons olive oil

⅔ cup (95 g) diced carrot

⅓ cup (35 g) chopped onion

8 ounces (227 g) plum tomatoes (about 2 tomatoes), chopped

2 small cloves or 1 large clove garlic, chopped

¾ cup (180 ml) chicken broth

3 sprigs fresh cilantro

⅓ cup (45 g) frozen green peas, thawed and drained (see Notas)

FOR SERVING

Sliced avocado

Salsa of choice

Warm corn tortillas

1. Rinse the rice thoroughly using a fine-mesh strainer, then place it in a medium bowl. Cover the rice with warm water and let soak for 15 minutes.

2. While the rice is soaking, season the chicken with salt and black pepper. In a large skillet, heat the oil over medium-low heat. Add the chicken and cook it for 7 to 8 minutes per side, until light golden. Transfer the chicken to a plate.

3. Drain the soaked rice using a fine-mesh strainer and shake it to remove any excess moisture. Before adding the rice to the pan the chicken was cooked in, make sure there is only about 1 tablespoon of oil in it, removing any excess oil and/or chicken fat. Add the drained rice to the pan and cook and stir over medium-high heat for 3 minutes, or until it is no longer transparent and starts to become slightly opaque. Add the carrot and onion and cook, stirring occasionally, for 3 more minutes.

4. Meanwhile, place the tomatoes, garlic cloves, and broth in a blender and process until smooth. Pour the tomato-garlic mixture over the rice and continue cooking until it starts boiling, then reduce the heat to low and season with salt. Add the chicken pieces back into the pan along with the cilantro and peas. Cover with the lid and continue to cook for 8 to 10 minutes, until the rice is well cooked and the chicken is fork-tender.

5. Remove the pan from the heat and let rest for about 5 more minutes before serving. (If you feel that the rice needs more liquid, add a little bit of warm chicken broth to it.)

6. Serve with avocado, salsa, and warm tortillas.

NOTAS

✴ *You can use any part of a chicken you prefer; just make sure that all the pieces are roughly the same size so they cook evenly. The cooking time will depend on what type of chicken it is (organic, pasture-raised, etc.), the size of the pieces, and the type of pan you use.*

✴ *During the resting time, some cooks cover the pan with a cloth napkin or kitchen towel to absorb any excess moisture from the rice.*

✴ *Other vegetables you can add to this dish in step 3 are chopped potatoes, celery, and green or red bell peppers.*

CREAMY CHIPOTLE CHICKEN

This is a more modern recipe, but one that has become a staple in many Mexican households. It's perfect for a midweek dinner, pairing wonderfully with a side of rice, pasta, or steamed vegetables, and you will be surprised by how quickly you can whip it up. The addition of the cream helps cool the heat from the chipotle peppers, making this a dish one that everyone can enjoy, even the little ones. Be sure to check the Notas for more creative ways to use this creamy chipotle sauce.

PREP TIME: 10 minutes	**COOK TIME:** 15 minutes	**YIELD:** 4 servings

1 pound (454 g) chicken breasts (see Notas), cut into 4 fillets

½ teaspoon garlic powder

½ teaspoon onion powder

Salt and black pepper

2 tablespoons vegetable oil

1 cup (240 ml) heavy cream

½ cup (120 ml) whole milk

½ cup (120 ml) chicken broth (see Notas)

2 chipotle peppers in adobo sauce (see Notas)

FOR GARNISHING AND SERVING

2 sprigs parsley

White rice

1. Season the chicken breasts with the garlic powder, onion powder, and salt and black pepper.

2. In a large skillet, heat the oil over medium-high heat. Add the chicken fillets and cook for about 3 minutes per side, or until slightly golden. Remove the chicken from the pan.

3. While the chicken is cooking, add the heavy cream, milk, broth, and chipotle peppers to a blender. Process for a couple of minutes until a fine texture.

4. Using a paper towel, clean up any excess oil from the skillet you cooked the chicken in. Turn the heat to medium-low and pour in the creamy chipotle sauce. Cook the sauce for 4 minutes, making sure to watch the heat; the sauce should be gently simmering, NOT boiling. (Too much heat will make the cream curdle.) Add the chicken fillets back into the pan and cook for 4 more minutes, or until cooked through, turning them if needed to achieve an even cooking.

5. Garnish with the parsley and serve with rice.

NOTAS

* *You can use other cuts of chicken, but the cooking time may vary.*

* *The addition of the 2 chipotle peppers may sound too spicy for some, but the cream and milk balance out the heat.*

* *This sauce is very versatile. You can use it with shrimp instead of chicken by first cooking the creamy chipotle sauce, then adding the raw shrimp and cooking for about 7 minutes, stirring occasionally, until they acquire a nice pink color. It can also be used for pasta or to make creamy chipotle enchiladas stuffed with shredded chicken.*

OLLA TAPADA

Olla tapada means "covered pot," and it is a dish that can be found in Oaxaca, Chiapas, Veracruz, and some regions of central Mexico. It's a hassle-free recipe that requires minimal effort. I like to serve it with rice and warm corn tortillas, although a warm crusty bread is also good for soaking up all those flavorful juices. While olla tapada is usually cooked in a clay pot, you can easily prepare it in any thick, sturdy pot that you have in your kitchen. This dish allows for many variations, so check out the Notas for some more ideas.

PREP TIME: 15 minutes	**COOK TIME:** 45 minutes	**YIELD:** 6 servings

6 chicken pieces (legs and thighs)

Salt and black pepper

2 tablespoons olive oil

3 medium carrots, peeled and cut into 1½-inch (4 cm) pieces

1 large chayote, peeled and cut into 1½-inch (4 cm) pieces

6 plum tomatoes, sliced (see Notas)

½ medium white onion, sliced

1 jalapeño pepper, cut in half

2 large cloves garlic, minced

10 pimiento-stuffed Spanish olives, sliced

2 teaspoons capers, rinsed

⅓ cup (50 g) raisins

2 bay leaves

2 sprigs thyme

½ stick Mexican cinnamon

1½ cups (360 ml) white wine or white vinegar (see Notas)

FOR SERVING

Warm corn tortillas, crusty bread (such as Bolillos on page 215), or white rice

1. Season the chicken pieces with salt and pepper.

2. Add the olive oil to a large pot, making sure it is spread all over. (This will help keep the chicken from sticking to the bottom.)

3. To form the first layer, place 3 pieces of the chicken on the bottom of the pot along with half of the carrots, chayote, tomatoes, onion, jalapeño, and garlic. Season the vegetables with salt and pepper. Add the remaining chicken, carrots, chayote, tomatoes, onion, jalapeño, and garlic to form the second layer. Season again with salt and pepper, then top with the olives, capers, raisins, bay leaves, thyme, and cinnamon stick. Pour the wine over all the ingredients. Do not stir.

4. Cover the pot with the lid and bring to a boil over medium-high heat. Once boiling, reduce the heat to a gentle simmer. Continue cooking for 45 to 50 minutes, until the chicken is cooked through and tender. Halfway through the cooking time, check to see if it needs more liquid. It usually will not need any because the chicken and vegetables will release their own liquids, but in case it does, add warm water or chicken broth, a few tablespoons at a time.

5. Serve with warm tortillas, crusty bread, or rice.

NOTAS

✖ *This dish is usually cooked with wine or vinegar, but some cooks use sherry wine. If you don't want to use wine or vinegar, you can substitute it with chicken broth.*

✖ *If you can't find ripe and juicy tomatoes, use a 28-ounce (794 g) can of whole peeled tomatoes.*

✖ *There are other variations of this dish that use green peas, potatoes, red peppers, plantains, oregano, saffron, and even achiote paste.*

POLLO A LAS FINAS HIERBAS

This is a simple but elegant dish that can be enjoyed year-round, but especially during the fall and winter months. Recipes like this one appear in the earliest Mexican cookbooks from the nineteenth century. The 1800s were marked by a heavy French influence on Mexican culture, which could be observed in the fashion, architecture, and cuisine of the time. Dishes such as *pollo a las finas hierbas* are an example of that cultural exchange, as are the many types of bread found at Mexican bakeries. This recipe was given to me by the owner of a small eatery when I lived in Monterrey in the state of Nuevo León. It's a comforting dish that I find myself making for my family almost every winter.

PREP TIME: 5 minutes	**COOK TIME:** 35 minutes	**YIELD:** 4 servings

4 chicken quarters (legs and thighs)

Salt and black pepper

2 tablespoons olive oil

¼ white onion, thickly sliced

2 cloves garlic, finely chopped

1½ cups (360 ml) dry white wine

½ teaspoon dried marjoram

½ teaspoon dried thyme

1 bay leaf

FOR GARNISHING AND SERVING

Fresh parsley

Steamed vegetables

Mashed potatoes

Warm crusty bread (such as Bolillos on page 215)

1. Season the chicken with salt and pepper.

2. In a large skillet, heat the oil over medium-high heat. Add the chicken to the pan and cook on both sides until lightly golden, about 4 minutes per side.

3. Add the onion and garlic to the pan and cook and stir until the onion starts to turn translucent, 2 to 3 minutes.

4. Pour in the wine and add the marjoram, thyme, and bay leaf. Bring to a boil, then reduce the heat to low and let simmer for about 20 minutes, or until the chicken is thoroughly cooked and tender. Taste and add more salt if needed.

5. Garnish with parsley and serve with some liquid from the pan along with steamed vegetables, mashed potatoes, and crusty bread.

NOTAS

✖ *I sometimes like to add ½ teaspoon of paprika in step 4 for extra flavor.*

✖ *You can also add ⅓ cup (80 ml) of heavy cream to the pan during the last 5 minutes of the cooking time, which will give it a nice creamy texture.*

MOLE VERDE

Compared to the festive and elaborate *mole poblano*, this *mole verde* is more casual and relaxed. It does not require as many ingredients or steps to make and is perfect for a Sunday dinner at home. Mole verde is sometimes referred to as *pipian verde* in some regions of Mexico, as it is related to the family of stews called *pipian*, which also have a sauce made using pumpkin seeds (*pepitas*). This sauce is earthy and nutty compared to other sauces that only have tomatillo. This stew can also be made with pork, or alternatively, you can substitute the chicken with potatoes, chayote, green beans, and nopales for a vegan version.

PREP TIME: 15 minutes	COOK TIME: 45 minutes	YIELD: 6 servings

CHICKEN (SEE NOTAS)

6 chicken pieces (legs, thighs, and/or breasts)

Salt

1 sprig fresh cilantro

½ small white onion

2 cloves garlic

SAUCE

6 medium tomatillos, husks removed

⅔ cup (90 g) roasted unsalted pumpkin seeds (pepitas)

½ cup (75 g) toasted sesame seeds

2 to 3 serrano peppers

2 large cloves garlic

½ small white onion, chopped

3 large romaine lettuce leaves, chopped

2 leaves fresh hoja santa, chopped

½ cup (20 g) chopped fresh cilantro

8 black peppercorns

2 whole cloves

FOR SERVING

White or red rice

Warm corn tortillas

1. To make the chicken: Place the chicken pieces in a large pot and season with salt. Add the cilantro sprig, onion half, garlic cloves, and just enough water to cover all the ingredients. Turn the heat to medium-high and bring to a boil, then reduce the heat to low and cover with the lid. Let gently simmer for about 30 minutes, or until cooked through but still firm.

2. While the chicken is cooking, make the sauce: Place the tomatillos in a medium saucepan, cover with water, and bring to a boil over high heat. Once boiling, reduce the heat to low and let simmer for 6 to 8 minutes, until the tomatillos are pale green and soft.

3. Drain the tomatillos and place in a blender along with the pumpkin seeds, sesame seeds, serrano peppers, garlic, chopped onion, lettuce, hoja santa, cilantro, peppercorns, cloves, and 1 cup (240 ml) of water (or chicken broth). Process until a very smooth sauce. (Depending on your blender, you may need to work in batches.)

4. Drain the chicken, reserving the broth and removing and discarding the cilantro, onion, and garlic, leaving only the chicken in the pot.

5. Pour the sauce over the chicken and cook over medium-low heat for about 3 minutes, stirring frequently to keep the sauce from sticking to the bottom. Once the sauce starts boiling, reduce the heat to low and let gently simmer for about 8 more minutes to allow all the flavors to combine (see Notas). Add the reserved chicken broth as needed to maintain a creamy texture.

6. Serve warm with rice and corn tortillas.

NOTAS

✖ *This recipe can also be made with pork. Use 2 pounds (907 g) of pork butt and a bay leaf when cooking it in step 1 instead of the sprig of cilantro.*

✖ *If you can't find fresh hoja santa, use 1 tablespoon of the dried version, finely crushed, which is also known as acuyo or momo, or completely eliminate it.*

✖ *Low heat is the key to keeping the sauce from curdling after you add it to the chicken. If it does curdle, add more chicken broth, stir, and cook for a few more minutes until the sauce has a creamy consistency.*

POLLO PIBIL

Savory and mouthwatering, this dish that has the same flavors as the famous Cochinita Pibil (page 113) but is made with chicken instead of pork. Just like the pork version, the chicken pieces are wrapped in banana leaves for cooking, but they are steamed instead of baked. In Yucatán, as well the rest of the country, it is more common to make *pollo pibil* for an everyday meal than *cochinita pibil*, which is generally reserved for weekends or special occasions.

PREP TIME: 10 minutes plus 30 minutes marinating time	**COOK TIME:** 45 minutes	**YIELD:** 6 servings

ACHIOTE MARINADE

2 large cloves garlic, chopped

½ block (1¼ ounces/50 g) achiote (annatto) paste

1½ cups (300 ml) fresh orange juice

¼ cup (60 ml) grapefruit juice or white vinegar

1 teaspoon salt

½ teaspoon black pepper

1 teaspoon dried Mexican oregano

¼ teaspoon ground cumin

MEAT

6 chicken leg quarters (about 3 pounds/1.4 kg) (see Notas on page 112)

Salt and black pepper

2 large banana leaves (if using frozen, thaw completely) (see Notas on page 112)

1 large tomato, thickly sliced

⅓ white or red onion, thinly sliced

6 fresh epazote leaves (see Notas on page 112)

1. To make the achiote marinade: Add the garlic cloves, achiote paste, orange and grapefruit juices, the 1 teaspoon salt, the ½ teaspoon black pepper, the oregano, cumin, and ¼ cup (60 ml) of water to a blender and process until a very smooth sauce.

2. To make the meat: Place the chicken in a large glass bowl and season with salt and pepper. Pour the achiote marinade over the chicken and use your hands to thoroughly mix and coat the pieces in the marinade. Cover the bowl with plastic wrap or a lid and let marinate in the refrigerator for at least 30 minutes.

3. Cut the banana leaves into ten 12-inch (30 cm) squares. Briefly pass the banana leaf pieces over the flame of your stove, making sure to pass the whole leaf over the flame. The texture of the leaf will become soft and pliable with the heat, and its surface will turn glossy. Afterward, rinse the leaf sections with warm water and dry them with a kitchen towel.

4. Take a piece of marinated chicken and place it in the center of a piece of banana leaf. Spoon some of the achiote marinade over the chicken and garnish with a slice of tomato, slices of onion, and an epazote leaf. Wrap the banana leaf around the chicken to form a rectangular package, like wrapping a tamal; fold the sides inward toward the center, then fold the bottom and top parts toward the center. Repeat this process to wrap the remaining chicken pieces.

(continued)

FOR SERVING

White rice

Frijoles Colados (page 162)

Warm corn tortillas

Pickled Red Onions (page 187) or
Pickled White Onion and Habanero
(page 186)

5. To steam, place a steamer rack inside a large stockpot. Add enough warm water up to the level of the steamer rack, then line the rack with 2 pieces of banana leaves. Place the chicken packages inside the steamer pot, arranging them on top of the banana leaves. Cover with the remaining 2 pieces of banana leaves (or aluminum foil), then cover the pot with the lid. Cook over medium-high heat for about 10 minutes, or until it comes to a boil, then reduce the heat to low and let simmer for 30 minutes. (You must make sure that the water at the bottom of the steamer does not run out, so refill it with hot water as needed to maintain the steam.) Be careful when opening or removing the lid because the steam will be very hot. Open one of the packages to check the chicken for doneness. It should be tender, moist, and have an internal temperature of at least 165°F (74°C); if it is not fully cooked, continue cooking for a few more minutes.

6. Remove the chicken from the banana leaves and serve with rice, warm tortillas, and pickled onions.

NOTAS

* *I prefer using 6 chicken leg quarters instead of a whole chicken. The quarters are easier to wrap, have more flavor, and provide equal portions.*

* *If you can't find banana leaves, aluminum foil can be used as an alternative for wrapping the chicken (you can also use both aluminum foil and banana leaves).*

* *If you can only find dried epazote, use ¼ teaspoon per chicken quarter, or skip it entirely.*

* *For an easier stovetop version, simply place the chicken pieces on a layer of banana leaves in a large Dutch oven and cover with the achiote marinade. Cover the chicken with more banana leaves, then cover with the lid and cook for 45 to 50 minutes over medium heat. If more liquid is needed, add some chicken broth to the Dutch oven.*

COCHINITA PIBIL

Pork Pibil

This is arguably the most popular recipe from the Yucatán region and an icon in Mexican gastronomy. It consists of pork meat that is marinated in an achiote sauce and wrapped in banana leaves before cooking. This is a kitchen-friendly adaptation of the original recipe, which is traditionally prepared by burying an entire pig in a pit and cooking it overnight. The pit is called a *pib* and is used to cook other Yucatán dishes, including those that are seasonal and ceremonial in nature. This process of cooking meats in an underground pit is very representative of this region of Mexico and dates back to Mayan times. The resulting cooked meat is extremely succulent and flavorful, due to the marinating time and the banana leaf wrapping. Although it's served with sides, the *cochinita* meat also makes a great filling for tacos, sopes, gorditas, and tortas.

PREP TIME: 15 minutes plus 2 hours marinating time	**COOK TIME:** 1 hour and 30 minutes (see Notas on page 115)	**YIELD:** 6 servings

ACHIOTE MARINADE

½ block (1¾ ounces/50 g) achiote (annatto) paste

1¾ cups (300 ml) fresh orange juice (see Notas page 115)

¼ cup (60 ml) grapefruit juice or white vinegar

2 large cloves garlic, chopped

½ teaspoon black pepper

Salt

MEAT

3 pounds (1.4 kg) boneless pork butt or shoulder (see Notas on page 115), cut into 2½-inch (6 cm) cubes

2 large banana leaves (if using frozen, thaw completely) (see Notas on page 115)

¼ cup (50 g) lard

½ white onion, thickly sliced

1 teaspoon dried Mexican oregano

2 allspice berries

1. To make the achiote marinade: Add the achiote paste, orange and grapefruit juices (or vinegar), garlic cloves, and black pepper to a blender. Season with salt and process until a very smooth sauce.

2. To prepare the meat: Place the pork in a large glass bowl, pour the achiote sauce over the meat, and use your hands to thoroughly mix and coat the pieces in the marinade. Cover the bowl with plastic wrap or a lid and refrigerate for 2 to 4 hours, or preferably overnight, to allow the flavors to infuse the meat and enhance its taste.

3. Preheat the oven to 350ºF (175ºC).

4. Cut the banana leaves into six 11- to 12-inch (28 to 30 cm) squares. Briefly pass the banana leaf pieces over the flame of your stove, making sure to pass the whole leaf over the flame. The texture of the leaf will become soft and pliable with the heat, and its surface will turn glossy. Afterward, rinse the leaf sections with warm water and dry them with a kitchen towel.

5. Line a roasting pan with aluminum foil. Arrange the banana leaves in the pan, overlapping them and allowing them to hang over the edges of the pan.

(continued)

FOR SERVING

Warm corn tortillas

Frijoles Colados (page 162)

**Pickled Red Onions (page 187) or
Pickled White Onion and Habanero
(page 186)**

6. Place the marinated pork over the banana leaves. Top the meat with the lard, onion, oregano, and allspice. Tightly wrap it like a package, folding the ends of the banana leaves over each other toward the center. Cover the roasting pan with a lid or aluminum foil.

7. Bake for 1½ hours, then remove from the oven. The meat should be tender at this point; if not, re-cover and bake for another 30 minutes.

8. Shred the meat and serve it with its released juices, some warm tortillas, frijoles coladas, and pickled onions.

NOTAS

✖ *You can also cook the pork in an Instant Pot or pressure cooker, lining the bottoms with banana leaves. The meat will take 45 minutes to 1 hour to cook on "Manual" setting on high pressure.*

✖ *This recipe is usually made using the juice of bitter oranges, but since it is not easily available some people substitute it with regular orange juice combined with vinegar to replicate its flavor. I prefer to combine orange juice with grapefruit juice instead.*

✖ *Traditionally this dish is made with pork butt or shoulder, but you can also use the loin or ribs.*

✖ *Although marinating the pork is highly recommended, there are some cooks who coat the meat with the marinade, then immediately cook it on the stovetop. This cooking method takes 45 minutes to 1 hour.*

✖ *If you can't find banana leaves, you can use only the aluminum foil or an oven bag. Also, instead of lining the roasting pan with aluminum foil, you can place the banana leaves inside an oven bag, add the ingredients, and close the bag according to the instructions on the packaging. The oven bag will help keep the meat extra moist.*

PORK IN TOMATO SAUCE

This is a recipe that I came up with in my kitchen one day when I wanted to make a stew for my family, and it has become a favorite dish of ours. Stews are very popular in Mexican cooking, due to how practical they are to make and how comforting they are as a meal. This recipe also shows how versatile a stew can be—you can add your favorite vegetables and herbs and use any type of meat. I use pork and the sauce is similar to other stews called *entomatado/a*, which have tomato-based sauces. I added some jalapeños and poblanos for heat and a splash of beer to enhance the flavors, a practice we use for many stews in the northern states.

PREP TIME: 10 minutes	**COOK TIME:** 1 hour	**YIELD:** 6 servings

MEAT

2 pounds (907 g) pork shoulder, cut into 1½-inch (4 cm) cubes

¼ medium onion

4 large cloves garlic

1 bay leaf

TOMATO SAUCE

⅓ white onion, finely chopped

2 large cloves garlic, minced

2 poblano peppers, seeds and veins removed and cut into strips

1 jalapeño pepper (see Notas), cut into strips

1 pound (454 g) plum tomatoes (4 or 5 tomatoes), diced

1 cup (240 ml) lager beer (see Notas)

Salt and black pepper

⅓ cup (15 g) chopped fresh cilantro

FOR SERVING

White rice

Warm corn tortillas

1. To make the meat: Place the pork in large pot or Dutch oven and cover with 4 cups (1 quart/950 ml) of water. Add the onion quarter, garlic cloves, and bay leaf and bring to a boil over medium-high heat. Once boiling, reduce the heat to bring the water to a gentle simmer and let cook for 30 minutes, or until the meat is fully cooked but still firm. (The water in the pan will reduce and the pork will release its fat.)

2. Remove and discard the onion, garlic and bay leaf. Let the meat brown in its fat, turning it occasionally, to have even browning. Once the meat is fully cooked (but still firm), make the sauce.

3. To make the sauce: Add the chopped onion and garlic to the meat pot, increase the heat to medium, and cook and stir until the onion is translucent, about 3 minutes, then add the poblano and jalapeño peppers and cook and stir for another 2 minutes.

4. Add the tomatoes and cook for 8 minutes, then pour in the beer and stir. Let the stew come to a boil, then reduce the heat to low.

5. Season with salt and black pepper and cover the pot with the lid. Let cook for another 15 minutes, or until all the flavors are blended together and the meat is tender enough to break apart when you insert a fork in it.

6. Stir in the chopped cilantro and serve with rice and warm tortillas.

NOTAS

✶ *You can cook this recipe without the jalapeño, or add more jalapeños for extra heat.*

✶ *Dark beers are commonly used in stews, but in this recipe I opted for a Mexican lager.*

✶ *You can add extra spices to the stew to give it even more flavor. In step 4, add 1 teaspoon of dried Mexican oregano, a pinch of ground cumin, and 1 or 2 whole cloves for a unique and delicious twist to this recipe.*

SPICY PORK SHORT RIBS

Country-style pork ribs are a true gem in Mexican cuisine. Sometimes referred to as *tablitas*, these short ribs can be found cooked in a variety of stews across the country, as well as grilled over fire. Whichever way you prepare them, their flavor will never disappoint. This particular stew has a spicy and flavorful sauce made with tomatoes and morita peppers. Morita peppers resemble chipotle peppers but boast a darker, shiny hue and are smaller in size.

PREP TIME: 10 minutes	COOK TIME: 1 hour and 20 minutes	YIELD: 6 servings

SHORT RIBS

2 pounds (907 g) country-style pork ribs, cut into small pieces

4 cloves garlic

1 bay leaf

¼ medium white onion

Salt

1 tablespoon vegetable oil (optional)

SAUCE

1½ pounds (680 g) plum tomatoes (about 6 tomatoes)

2 or 3 morita peppers (see Nota)

¼ medium white onion

1 clove garlic

⅓ teaspoon dried thyme

⅓ teaspoon dried marjoram

Salt and black pepper

FOR SERVING

White rice

Warm corn tortillas

> **NOTA** *You can use chipotle or árbol peppers as a substitute for the morita peppers, and the stew will still come out tasting incredibly delicious.*

1. **To make the short ribs:** Place the ribs in a large stockpot or Dutch oven and add the 4 garlic cloves, bay leaf, onion quarter, and enough water (6 to 8 cups/1 to 1½ quarts/1.4 to 1.9 L) to cover the ingredients. Season with salt and bring to a boil over high heat. Once boiling, reduce the heat to low to gently simmer and cook for 40 to 50 minutes, until tender. (As the pork cooks, you may notice a gray foam forming on the surface of the broth; skim it off with a spoon and discard.)

2. While the short ribs are cooking, make the sauce: Place the tomatoes, morita peppers, onion quarter, and the garlic clove in a medium saucepan with enough water to cover the ingredients. Let cook over medium heat for about 20 minutes, or until the peppers are soft. Drain, transfer the cooked ingredients to a blender, and process until a smooth sauce.

3. Once the ribs are cooked, drain all the liquid from the pot, reserving it, and remove and discard the garlic, onion, and bay leaf. Let the ribs brown in their own fat in the same pot over medium-low heat to enhance its flavor. If the meat does not release enough fat, add 1 tablespoon of vegetable oil.

4. Add the sauce to the pot with the ribs through a fine-mesh strainer to remove any pepper skins. Crumble the dried thyme and marjoram with your fingers and add them to the sauce. Stir everything together and season with salt and black pepper. Let the stew simmer for 10 more minutes. If the sauce seems too thick, add a couple of tablespoons of the cooking broth from the ribs to thin it slightly.

5. Serve with rice and warm tortillas.

TORTA DE JAMÓN

Mexican Ham Sandwich

In Mexico, a *torta* is a sandwich that is prepared with a thick bread and is similar to a sub or hoagie in the United States. The breads commonly used to make tortas are the telera and bolillo styles. The fillings and preparation for a torta are practically endless, and you can find different styles of tortas being served throughout Mexico. For example, in the south, there are tortas made with Cochinita Pibil (page 113); in central Mexico, tortas are often made with milanesa (breaded cutlets); and in the north, they are filled with Chorizo (page 122) or Chilorio (page 48). But the type of torta that you will find everywhere in the country is the classic *torta de jamón*. Like most other tortas, this one is affordable, practical, and easy to carry, making it a popular lunch choice for workers and students across Mexico. Throughout the country, it is common to see small stands selling tortas near schools, offices, hospitals, and government buildings. Given that it's such a popular sandwich, everyone has their own way of making it, so I hope you try my recipe, and then adjust it to make it your own.

PREP TIME: 10 minutes	**COOK TIME:** 5 minutes	**YIELD:** 1 torta

1 Bolillo (page 215) or telera (or a 6-inch/15-cm baguette or a Kaiser roll)

2 tablespoons black refried beans (see Notas)

1 tablespoon mayonnaise

¼ avocado, sliced

2 slices baked ham

2 slices queso fresco

2 slices tomato

2 slices white onion

1 tablespoon butter, softened

FOR SERVING

Pickled Jalapeño Peppers and Carrots (page 184)

1. Heat a comal over medium heat.

2. Cut the bread in half lengthwise and spread the bottom half of the bread with the refried beans and the top half with the mayonnaise.

3. Place the avocado slices, then the ham on top of the bottom half of the bread, followed by the queso fresco, onion, and tomato. Finally, place the other half of bread on top.

4. Melt the butter on the hot comal, then place the torta on the comal and allow it to warm and crisp up, about 2 minutes. Using a large spatula, flip the torta over to warm the other side for 2 to 3 minutes. (I like to let the bread get a little crispy). Remove the torta from the comal and cut it in half.

5. Serve with a side of pickled jalapeños and carrots.

NOTAS

✻ *To make the refried beans, heat 1 tablespoon of vegetable oil or lard in a small skillet over medium-high heat. Stir in 2 tablespoons of chopped onion and cook and stir until golden brown. Add 1 cup (175 g) of cooked black beans and gently mash them using a bean or potato masher until a fine puree. Season with salt.*

✻ *If adding lettuce, place it on top of the ham along with the tomato and onion.*

✻ *While they are not usually considered an antojito, tortas can be found at many city street food stands being sold alongside tacos, sopes, and gorditas.*

HOMEMADE CHORIZO

Mexican *chorizo* gets its distinct flavor from a blend of spices, herbs, and dried peppers that are generally consistent throughout Mexico, although there are some regions that have their own varieties of chorizo. This recipe was given to me by one of my younger sisters while she was studying food engineering in college and had to make chorizo for a class project. There are many ways that chorizo is used in Mexico, from the classic Huevos con Chorizo (page 27) to the famous Queso Fundido (page 165). It can also be used as a filling for tacos, tortas, sopes, and more.

PREP TIME: 1 hour plus 24 hours curing time	**YIELD:** 20 chorizo links

6 guajillo peppers (see Notas), seeds and veins removed

3 ancho peppers (see Notas), seeds and veins removed

3 tablespoons paprika

2 bay leaves

½ teaspoon black pepper

1 teaspoon ground cumin

2 teaspoons dried Mexican oregano

½ teaspoon dried marjoram

½ teaspoon coriander seeds

½ teaspoon dried thyme

6 whole cloves, chopped

2 allspice berries

6 cloves garlic, chopped

1½ tablespoons salt

½ cup (120 ml) white vinegar

2 pounds (907 g) ground pork shoulder or butt (see Notas)

6 ounces (170 g) ground pork belly (see Notas)

80 inches (2 m) sausage casings (see Notas)

Butcher's twine or strips of corn husks, to tie the chorizo

1. Place the guajillo and ancho peppers in a large bowl with warm water. Let them soak for at least 20 minutes, or until soft. Drain the peppers and place them in a blender along with the paprika, bay leaves, black pepper, cumin, oregano, marjoram, coriander, thyme, cloves, allspice, garlic, salt, and vinegar. Process until a very fine and smooth sauce.

2. Place the ground pork and pork belly in a large nonaluminum bowl. Add the pepper mixture to the meat and mix until well combined. (You can cook a very small patty of chorizo to taste the flavor and adjust the seasonings to your liking.)

3. Place the casings in a medium bowl and soak in warm water until soft and pliable, at least 30 minutes. After this, run lukewarm water through the casings to remove any salt.

4. Cut the casings into 3- to 4-foot-long (0.9 to 1.2 m) pieces, tying a double knot at on end of each piece, to make it easier to stuff. Place the open end of the casing onto the tip of a funnel (if stuffing by hand) or on the nozzle of a sausage stuffer. Pull back all but 3 inches (7.5 cm) of the casing onto the funnel tip/nozzle.

5. Start by gently pressing small portions of the chorizo mixture through the tip/nozzle, supporting the casing with your other hand. Do not pack the sausage too tight because that could cause the casing to burst. It is important to leave some space in the casing for when you twist or tie it to form the chorizo links. Also leave 3 inches (7.5 cm) at the other end of the casing in case you need to adjust the size of the chorizos.

6. Once the whole length of the casing has been stuffed, place it on a counter or table. Begin to form the chorizo links by gently pinching the sausage where you want to divide them and twisting the sausage there to break them up. Proceed to tie this spot with butcher's twine or thin strips of corn husks. Repeat until you have divided the whole casing into links.

7. Using a toothpick, prick a small hole into each link to release any air that has been trapped in the casing. Hang the chorizo in a dry room, free of dust and insects. (You can cover the chorizo with a cheesecloth while it cures.) Cure for 24 hours (some of the vinegar may drip from the chorizo during the curing process). After the curing time, the chorizo is ready to cook or store. The chorizo will stay fresh for up to 5 days in the fridge; after that, store it in the freezer.

NOTAS

* *If you can only find the powdered form of guajillo and ancho peppers, substitute 2 teaspoons of guajillo powder for each guajillo pepper and 3 teaspoons of ancho powder for each ancho pepper and add them to the blender in step 1.*

* *To make the chorizo spicy, add 1 or 2 dried chipotle or árbol peppers in step 1.*

* *If you can't find ground pork, you can finely chop the meat with a sharp knife. Before preparing the chorizo mixture, ensure that the meat is thoroughly chilled. This will make it easier to handle and work with when stuffing it in the casing.*

* *If you're not going to stuff the chorizo into casings, let the chorizo mixture cure in the refrigerator for a day, then stir the mixture and store it in medium-size freezer bags. It will freeze well for months.*

* *Once you make your first batch of homemade chorizo, feel free to adjust the seasonings in this recipe to your liking. Some people prefer it with more herbs or spices. Make it your own!*

PESCADILLAS
Crispy Fish Tacos

Pescadillas have their origins in the Pacific Coast region of Mexico, in states such as Sinaloa, Guerrero, and Oaxaca, where they are served at seafood restaurants or sold at stands by the beach. These crunchy tacos are great for pool parties or family cookouts, especially when accompanied with some ice-cold beer. In many parts of Mexico, pescadillas are usually made with a fish called *cazón* (dogfish), a type of small shark. It has a lot of meat, but cazón is not easy to find everywhere, so I like to use cod. It cooks quickly and is easy to shred, making it an excellent option for this recipe.

PREP TIME: 20 minutes	**COOK TIME:** 40 minutes	**YIELD:** 12 tacos

FILLING

2 tablespoons olive or vegetable oil

⅓ cup (40 g) finely chopped onion

1 serrano pepper, finely chopped

1 clove garlic, minced

3 plum tomatoes, diced

1 pound (454 g) cod or 3 cans
(7 ounces/198 g each) tuna, drained
(see Notas on page 126)

½ teaspoon dried Mexican oregano

½ teaspoon dried thyme

Pinch of ground cumin

1 bay leaf

Salt and black pepper

PESCADILLAS

12 corn tortillas

2 cups (480 ml) vegetable oil

1. To make the filling: In a medium skillet, heat the 2 tablespoons oil over medium-high heat. Add the onion and serrano pepper and cook and stir until the onion is translucent, about 3 minutes. Add the garlic and cook and stir for 1 minute. Add the tomatoes, then cover the pan with the lid and let the tomatoes cook for 3 minutes.

2. Remove the lid and place the fish in the tomato sauce. Cover again and keep cooking for about 6 minutes; by this time, the fish will start to break apart. With the help of a spoon, separate the fish into small pieces.

3. Stir in the oregano, thyme, cumin, and bay leaf and cook for 4 minutes, uncovered, or until there is no liquid left in the pan. Stir well and season with salt and pepper. (It is important that you allow all the liquid to evaporate because you do not want any liquid to spill out of the pescadillas when frying them.) Remove the pan from the heat and let cool.

4. To make the pescadillas: Warm the tortillas on a hot comal preheated over medium heat for just enough time on each side to make them soft and pliable. (Cold tortillas tend to break, so do not skip this step.) Transfer the warm tortillas to a plate, cover with a cloth napkin or kitchen towel.

(continued)

TOPPINGS

3 cups (285 g) shredded cabbage

1 avocado, sliced

Thinly sliced radish (optional)

Spicy salsa of choice

Lime wedges

5. In a medium skillet, heat the oil over medium heat. While the oil is heating up, form the pescadillas by spreading about 1½ tablespoons of the filling in the center of a tortilla, making sure that the filling does not reach the edge of the tortilla. Fold the tortilla to close it, then insert two toothpicks near the top edges of the tortilla, threading each toothpick to go through the other side of the tortilla and back out. Try to cover a wide section of the tortilla with each toothpick; they should not touch the filling in the center of the tortilla. Repeat this step with the remaining tortillas, filling, and toothpicks.

6. Cook the pescadillas, in batches, for 4 to 5 minutes per side, until golden brown. Transfer to a paper towel–lined plate to absorb any excess oil.

7. Serve the pescadillas with the shredded cabbage, avocado slices, radish slices (if using), salsa for topping, and lime wedges for squeezing.

NOTAS

✱ *You can use other types of white fish for this recipe, such as tilapia, halibut, haddock, sea bass, or sole. Canned tuna is also a popular choice, so I have added the amount needed in the ingredients list. To choose the best fish for these tacos, make sure the fish is firm, does not have a strong odor, and is not leaking any liquids.*

✱ *The fish is usually cooked first by boiling it in water, but I like to add it directly to the tomato sauce to keep the flavors of the fish in the sauce, saving a step in the cooking process.*

✱ *If you like Pickled Red Onions (page 187), they make an excellent complement to this dish.*

✱ *The filling can also be used as a topping for baked tostadas, making a healthy meal option.*

✱ *To store any leftovers, place them in an airtight container in the refrigerator for up to 3 days. You can reheat the pescadillas in an oven preheated to 350°F (175°F) for about 10 minutes.*

EMPANADAS DE ATÚN

Tuna Empanadas

This recipe is an homage to my hometown of Tampico, where we love seafood and have come up with many creative ways to use it. The filling for these empanadas is usually prepared with other types of fish, but I use canned tuna because it is easily available and the results are always tasty. Something that makes these empanadas unique is the orange color of the masa dough. It is achieved by using a simple ancho pepper sauce and adding it to the dough (see Notas on page 129). Don't worry; it doesn't make the dough spicy. There are some regions in Mexico where the ancho pepper is known as "chile color," because it's only used to add color to dishes.

PREP TIME: 20 minutes	**COOK TIME:** 20 minutes	**YIELD:** 12 empanadas

FILLING

2 tablespoons vegetable oil

⅔ cup (85 g) finely chopped white onion

1 clove garlic, minced

1½ cups (270 g) diced tomato

2 cans (7 ounces/198 g each) tuna (see Notas), drained

2 tablespoons chopped fresh parsley

Salt and black pepper

DOUGH

1 ancho pepper, soaked in hot water for 25 minutes

2 cups (224 g) masa harina

1½ cups (360 ml) warm water (see Notas)

1 teaspoon salt

½ cup (120 ml) vegetable oil

1. To make the filling: In a medium skillet, heat the 2 tablespoons oil over medium-high heat. Add the onion and cook and stir until translucent, about 3 minutes. Add the garlic and cook and stir for 1 minute.

2. Stir in the tomato and cook thoroughly until its juices have been reduced, 8 to 10 minutes. Remove the pan from the heat and stir in the tuna and parsley. Season with salt and black pepper and set aside to cool.

3. To make the dough: Place the soaked ancho pepper in a blender along with 2½ tablespoons of its soaking water and process until a smooth sauce.

4. In a large bowl, combine the masa harina, warm water, and salt and mix well. Add 2½ tablespoons of the ancho sauce to the dough. Knead the dough until you have a uniform texture. If the dough feels dry, add more water, a spoonful at a time, until the dough is soft and manageable, like play dough; it does not need to be sticky. This dough tends to be dry, so add more water if needed. (If you live in a place with lots of humidity, the masa dough will not need too much water.) Cover the dough with a moistened cloth napkin or kitchen towel; this will help to keep the dough moist. Divide the dough into 12 equal-size balls and cover with the moistened cloth.

(continued)

TOPPINGS

2 cups (190 g) finely shredded cabbage

3 radishes, thinly sliced

Spicy salsa of your choice

Pickled Red Onions (page 187)

1 avocado, sliced (optional)

Lime wedges

5. Place a ball of dough between two 7 x 7-inch (18 x 18 cm) plastic sheets cut from a freezer bag. Using a tortilla press or a heavy glass pie dish, press down to form a tortilla shape, then remove the top plastic sheet. Place about 1 tablespoon of the tuna filling on top of the tortilla in the center. With the help of the bottom plastic sheet, slowly fold the tortilla in half and seal the edges well, using your fingers to lightly press, starting from the middle and working outward. (It is important to seal the edges well, because if the filling leaks out when frying, it can cause the oil to splatter.) Transfer to a tray and cover with a moistened cloth napkin or kitchen towel while repeating this process with the remaining dough balls and filling.

6. In a large skillet, heat the ½ cup (120 ml) oil over medium-high heat. Lower an empanada into the hot oil and cook until golden and slightly crispy, about 2 minutes per side, though the cooking time may vary depending on the oil temperature (you can fry more than one at a time; just don't overcrowd the pan). Remove from the pan with a slotted spoon and transfer to a cooling rack or a paper towel–lined plate to absorb any excess oil. Continue frying the rest of the empanadas. Let cool a little.

7. Serve with the shredded cabbage, radish slices, salsa, pickled onions, avocado (if using), and lime wedges for squeezing.

NOTAS

✖ *It's not necessary to add the ancho pepper salsa to the dough.*

✖ *If you have some leftover cooked fish, you can use 1½ cups (200 g) of shredded fish instead of the tuna.*

✖ *Store leftover empanadas in an airtight container in the refrigerator for about 3 days. To reheat, place them on a comal preheated over medium heat, turning them occasionally, until they are completely warm.*

TILAPIA A LA VERACRUZANA

Tilapia Veracruz-Style

This recipe is an adaption of an iconic dish from the port city of Veracruz, called "red snapper Veracruz-style." The red snapper is traditionally cooked and served whole, but because whole red snapper is not easy to find everywhere, I like to use fish fillets instead. The use of capers, olives, and herbs make this a vibrant and aromatic dish with a unique character, and it is just one of the many magical flavor combinations you can experience in the Veracruz region.

PREP TIME: 10 minutes	**COOK TIME:** 20 minutes	**YIELD:** 4 servings

2 tablespoons olive oil (see Notas)

½ medium white onion, diced

2 cloves garlic, finely chopped

4 ripe, juicy Roma tomatoes (see Notas), diced

1 bay leaf

1 small sprig fresh thyme or ½ teaspoon dried thyme

½ teaspoon dried Mexican oregano, finely crushed

½ teaspoon dried marjoram

⅓ cup (40 g) whole or sliced pimiento-stuffed Spanish olives (see Notas)

1½ tablespoons capers, drained and rinsed

¼ cup (60 ml) dry white wine (see Notas)

Salt and black pepper

4 tilapia or any white fish fillets (about 1½ pounds/680 g)

FOR GARNISHING AND SERVING

Pickled Jalapeño Peppers and Carrots (page 184) (optional)

Pickled banana peppers (optional)

White rice, pasta, or warm crusty bread

1. In a large skillet, heat the oil over medium heat. Add the onion and garlic and cook until the onion is slightly translucent, 2 to 3 minutes. Stir in the tomatoes, cover the pan with the lid, and cook for 8 minutes to allow the tomatoes to release their juices.

2. Remove the lid and add the bay leaf, thyme, oregano, marjoram, olives, capers, and white wine. Season with salt and pepper and cook, covered, for 4 more minutes to allow the flavors to blend and the sauce to reduce. Add the fish fillets, spoon some tomato sauce over them, and cover with the lid again. Cook for 5 to 6 minutes, then remove the pan from the heat to avoid overcooking the fish. (To check the doneness of the fish fillets, gently insert a fork into a fillet and pull it back out; if the fish flakes easily without resistance, that means it is ready to eat.)

3. Garnish with pickled peppers (if using) and serve with white rice, pasta, or crusty bread.

NOTAS

✳ *Spanish olive oil is used when cooking this dish (and others like it) in Veracruz.*

✳ *If you can't find ripe and juicy tomatoes, use canned tomatoes instead.*

✳ *Manzanilla olives are the traditional olives used for this dish, but any green olives will work.*

✳ *You can substitute chicken broth for the white wine.*

PESCADO AL MOJO DE AJO
Garlic Fish Fillets

Pescado al mojo de ajo is a delightful way of preparing a fish fillet. It's surprisingly delicious despite how simple it is to make and how few ingredients it requires. In Mexico, when a dish is described as *al mojo de ajo*, or *al ajillo*, it means that it is prepared with garlic as the key ingredient. You can find seafood restaurants preparing fish, shrimp, and even octopus in this way. I like to serve this dish with rice and a salad or steamed vegetables.

PREP TIME: 10 minutes	**COOK TIME:** 10 minutes	**YIELD:** 4 servings

1½ pounds (680 g) tilapia fillets (see Notas)

Salt and black pepper

Juice of 1 lime

¼ cup (60 ml) vegetable oil (or a mix of half olive oil and half vegetable oil)

6 cloves garlic, thinly sliced

2 tablespoons all-purpose flour (optional; see Notas)

FOR GARNISHING AND SERVING

3 tablespoons finely chopped parsley

White rice

Lettuce salad

1 tablespoon salted butter (optional)

1. Season the fish fillets with salt and pepper and the lime juice.

2. In a large nonstick skillet, heat the oil over low heat. Add the garlic and cook and stir for a few seconds, until a light-golden color (watch carefully). Remove the garlic promptly from the pan (or they will have a bitter taste).

3. If using the flour, lightly dust the fillets with a fine coating. Place the skillet the garlic was cooked in over medium-high heat. Once the oil is hot, add the fish to the pan and cook on both sides, 2 to 3 minutes per side for fillets around ⅓ inch (8.5 mm) thick and 4 to 5 minutes for thicker fillets. Do not flip the fish until the bottom side is golden and cooked. Transfer the fillets to a paper towel-lined plate to absorb any excess oil.

4. Garnish the fillets with the chopped parsley and fried garlic slices and serve with rice and salad. I like to add a dab of butter to each fillet when serving.

NOTAS

* *You can use a variety of types of fish for this recipe, including cod, mahi-mahi, and sole.*

* *This recipe typically doesn't use flour, but if you don't have experience of cooking fish, or do not have a nonstick skillet, the flour will help you obtain golden fish fillets and keep them from sticking to the pan or breaking while cooking.*

CEVICHE

This recipe is one of the most popular ways to make *ceviche* in the Gulf of Mexico. I've tried this dish in many different regions of Mexico, and the same basics always apply: fish, onion, tomato, serrano pepper, cilantro, and lime juice. Ceviche can also be made with other seafood, such as shrimp, octopus, crab, clams, or a combination of these. This ceviche can be served as an appetizer or enjoyed as a main meal.

PREP TIME: 10 minutes plus 30 minutes marinating time	**YIELD:** 6 servings

1 pound (454 g) fish fillets (tilapia, red snapper, or sea bass; see Notas), cut into ½-inch (13 mm) cubes

⅓ cup (80 ml) fresh lime juice

Salt

3 large plum tomatoes, finely chopped

2 serrano peppers or 1 large jalapeño, finely chopped

1 medium onion, finely chopped

1 cup (40 g) finely chopped fresh cilantro

½ teaspoon dried Mexican oregano, crushed

FOR GARNISHING AND SERVING

1 avocado, diced

⅓ cup (40 g) sliced pimiento-stuffed Spanish olives (optional)

¼ cup (60 ml) olive oil

Saltine crackers or tortilla chips (see Notas)

Ketchup (optional; see Notas)

Tabasco sauce (optional)

1. Place the fish in a glass bowl, coat with the lime juice and salt, cover, and leave to marinate in the refrigerator for at least 20 minutes and up to 2 hours.

2. Drain the marinade from the bowl, leaving just a couple of tablespoons of the liquid to keep the fish moist, then stir in the tomatoes, peppers, onion, cilantro, and oregano. Taste the liquid, then add more salt if needed. Let everything marinate in the refrigerator for another 10 minutes.

3. To serve, fill cocktail glasses or small individual bowls with the ceviche, garnish with the avocado and olives (if using), and drizzle some olive oil over the top. Serve with saltine crackers or tortilla chips and, if desired, ketchup and Tabasco for drizzling.

NOTAS

* *In addition to the fish mentioned in the ingredients, you can also make this recipe using any other type of fish that has a firm texture.*

* *You can also serve the ceviche with whole tostadas instead of tortilla chips.*

* *Some people like to add a bit of ketchup to their ceviche, stirring it in just before garnishing. You can add it to the whole bowl of ceviche or to an individual serving, if you like.*

COCTEL DE CAMARÓN

Shrimp Cocktail

Just like the beloved Ceviche (page 134), the shrimp cocktail holds a special place in the hearts of seafood enthusiasts in Mexico. With its refreshing flavors and attractive presentation, it has become a classic menu item at restaurants in the coastal towns. This delicious cocktail can serve as a great appetizer or light meal, especially in the summer.

PREP TIME: 10 minutes plus 30 minutes chilling time	**COOK TIME:** 2 minutes	**YIELD:** 4 servings

SHRIMP

¼ white onion

6 cloves garlic

1 bay leaf

1 small sprig fresh thyme or ½ teaspoon dried thyme

1½ pounds (680 g) raw large shrimp (see Notas), heads, shells, and tails removed and deveined

COCKTAIL SAUCE

1 cup (240 ml) ketchup

¼ cup (60 ml) fresh lime juice

2 tablespoons olive oil

Salt and black pepper

FOR GARNISHING AND SERVING

⅓ cup (15 g) finely chopped fresh cilantro

1 cup (125 g) finely chopped red onion

1 serrano pepper (see Notas), finely chopped

1 avocado, diced

Bottled hot sauce of choice

Olive oil

Saltine crackers or corn tostadas (optional)

4 to 6 lime wedges

1. To make the shrimp: Place the white onion quarter, garlic cloves, bay leaf, and thyme in a large saucepan along with 6 cups (1½ quarts/1.4 L) of water over medium-high heat and bring to a boil. Once boiling, add the shrimp and cook for 2 minutes, or until the shrimp curl up and acquire a pink color. Remove the pot from the heat. Use a strainer to remove the shrimp, reserving the cooking broth. Let the shrimp cool for at least 30 minutes, or until they are completely cool. (You can also place the shrimp in a bath of ice water to speed up the cooling process.)

2. Meanwhile, make the cocktail sauce: In a large bowl, combine the ketchup, lime juice, olive oil, and 1¼ cups (300 ml) of the reserved shrimp broth until well combined. (If the sauce is too thick, add a little more shrimp broth.) Season with salt and black pepper.

3. Once the shrimp have cooled, divide them among four cocktail glasses. Pour some of the cocktail sauce over the shrimp, then top with the cilantro, red onion, serrano pepper, and avocado. Serve alongside the bottled hot sauce, olive oil, saltine crackers or tostadas (if using), and lime wedges for squeezing.

NOTAS

✽ *This recipe can also be made using 1 pound of already cooked, peeled, and deveined shrimp. Use 1 bottle (8 ounces/236 ml) of clam juice as a substitute for the shrimp broth in step 2.*

✽ *You can substitute the serrano pepper with a habanero or jalapeño pepper.*

ENCREMADAS
Cream Enchiladas

The sauce for these enchiladas is made with tomatillos, serrano peppers, and sour cream, resulting in a rich sauce that balances out its own heat. Commonly eaten for brunch or lunch, *encremadas* are often served with a side of black beans and a piece of grilled meat, usually skirt steak (also called *fajita*). This recipe hails from a region of Mexico called La Huasteca, which spans parts of Tamaulipas, Veracruz, and San Luis Potosí. Besides having many natural wonders, the Huasteca region is known for its delicious cuisine, including its colorful assortment of enchilada varieties.

PREP TIME: 10 minutes	**COOK TIME:** 20 minutes	**YIELD:** 4 servings

4 medium tomatillos (about 12 ounces/340 g)

3 serrano peppers or 1 jalapeño pepper

1 clove garlic

4 tablespoons vegetable oil, divided

12 medium-size corn tortillas

1¼ cups (300 ml) sour cream

FOR GARNISHING

1 cup (120 g) crumbled queso fresco

½ avocado, sliced

¼ onion, thinly sliced

NOTAS

✽ *Do not overcook the tomatillos (after the water comes to a boil, reduce the heat to a gentle simmer). If your tomatillo sauce does end up being bitter, add a pinch of sugar.*

✽ *If you are not used to spicy foods, use only 1 or 2 serrano peppers.*

1. Place the tomatillos, serrano peppers, and garlic clove in a medium saucepan and cover with about 4 cups (1 quart/950 ml) of water. Cook over medium heat for about 15 minutes, or until the tomatillos and serrano peppers are cooked through. Drain, reserving the cooking water and letting the tomatillos slightly cool.

2. Meanwhile, in a medium skillet, heat 2 tablespoons of the oil over medium-high heat. Lightly fry the tortillas, one at a time, on both sides, adding the remaining 2 tablespoons oil as needed. Do not let the tortillas get crispy; just fry them until they are soft and pliable. Transfer to a paper towel–lined plate.

3. Place the cooked tomatillos, peppers, and garlic in a blender along with ¼ cup (60 ml) of the cooking water and process until a smooth sauce. Add the sour cream to the blender and process again until a fine, light-green sauce.

4. Remove any excess oil from the skillet that the tortillas were fried in. Pour the sauce into the skillet and warm it over medium-low heat until it has a very creamy consistency. (If the salsa is reducing and getting thicker while warming it, add a little bit of the cooking water from the tomatillos.)

5. Dip each tortilla into the warm salsa, then, with the help of a large spatula or kitchen tongs, fold the tortilla in half and place it on the serving plates, placing 3 enchiladas on each plate. Garnish the encremadas with the queso fresco and avocado and onion slices.

ENFRIJOLADAS

Enfrijoladas are similar to enchiladas, with the difference being that they have a bean sauce instead of a tomato- or pepper-based sauce. The name *enfrijolada* comes from the word *frijol*, which means "bean." Most of the time, the bean sauce is made with black beans, but there are some enfrijoladas that are made with pinto beans. They can be filled with chicken, cheese, or chorizo.

PREP TIME: 20 minutes	**COOK TIME:** 15 minutes	**YIELD:** 8 enfrijoladas

2 cups cooked black (370 g) or pinto beans (342 g)

½ cup (120 ml) bean cooking broth

6 tablespoons vegetable oil, divided

Salt (optional)

8 corn tortillas

2 cups (300 g) cooked shredded chicken or 6 ounces (170 g) Mexican chorizo (about 2 medium-size chorizo links), casings removed, crumbled, and cooked, warmed

FOR GARNISHING AND SERVING

½ cup (120 ml) Mexican crema

½ cup (60 g) crumbled queso fresco or panela

¼ cup (30 g) thinly sliced onion (optional)

Chopped fresh cilantro (optional)

Sliced avocado (optional)

1. Add the cooked beans to a blender along with the bean cooking broth and process until a smooth sauce. (If the sauce is too thick, add water or chicken broth and blend again until it has the consistency of a creamy salsa.)

2. In a large skillet, heat 2 tablespoons of the oil over medium-high heat. Add the bean puree and simmer for about 3 minutes. Season with salt (if needed). Set aside and keep warm on the stovetop over very low heat.

3. In a separate large skillet, heat the remaining 4 tablespoons oil over medium-high heat. Using kitchen tongs, quickly fry the tortillas, one at a time, on each side for a few seconds. You do not want the tortillas to be crispy, so only cook them long enough to still be pliable (this step is done very quickly). Drain each tortilla with a slotted spoon and transfer to a paper towel-lined plate. Cover the fried tortillas with aluminum foil to keep them warm.

4. Using the kitchen tongs, dip each tortilla in the bean sauce, then transfer to a plate. Add a spoonful of the filling (shredded chicken or chorizo) on the center of the tortilla, then roll it closed or fold it in half. Repeat with the remaining tortillas and filling.

5. Spoon a little more of the bean sauce over the enfrijoladas, then drizzle with crema and top with cheese and some of the crumbled chorizo (if using).

6. If desired, serve with the onion, cilantro, and/or avocado.

NOTAS

✖ *To make the bean sauce more flavorful, slightly toast an avocado leaf on a comal, then add it to the blender in step 1. If you want to make the sauce spicy, add 1 chopped jalapeño pepper or 2 chopped árbol peppers to the blender in step 1. If using árbol peppers, slightly toast them on a comal first.*

✖ *The main ingredients of this dish (the bean sauce and cooked chicken or chorizo) can be prepared ahead, refrigerated, and warmed before assembling.*

ESPAGUETI ROJO

Spaghetti in Tomato Sauce

This is the most common way that spaghetti is eaten in Mexico. It is enjoyed by people of all ages, especially children. Besides being made at home, *espagueti rojo* is also commonly available at neighborhood eateries called *cocinas economicas* (economic kitchens), which have a small dining area, but primarily sell food to go and offer an assortment of homestyle Mexican dishes.

PREP TIME: 15 minutes	**COOK TIME:** 20 minutes	**YIELD:** 4 servings

PASTA

1 teaspoon salt

8 ounces (227 g) uncooked spaghetti

SAUCE

2 pounds (907 g) ripe, juicy plum tomatoes (about 7 tomatoes; see Notas)

½ cup (65 g) finely chopped white onion

1 clove garlic

1 tablespoon vegetable oil

¼ teaspoon dried Mexican oregano

2 teaspoons chicken bouillon granules

Salt

FOR GARNISHING

¼ cup (60 ml) Mexican crema or sour cream (see Notas)

½ cup (60 g) crumbled queso fresco

Flat-leaf parsley leaves

1. To make the pasta: Place 8 cups (2 quarts/1.9 L) of water in a medium pot and bring to a boil over medium-high heat. Once boiling, add the salt, then add the pasta. Once the water comes back to a boil, let the pasta cook for about 8 minutes for al dente pasta, then drain.

2. While the pasta is cooking, make the sauce: Place the tomatoes in a large pot, cover with water, and bring to a boil over medium-high heat. Once boiling, cook the tomatoes for 8 minutes, then remove from the pot. Let cool a bit, then remove and discard their skins.

3. Place the tomatoes in a blender along with the onion and garlic and process until a smooth sauce.

4. In a large skillet, heat the oil over medium heat. Pour the tomato sauce into the pan through a fine-mesh strainer and cook for about 2 minutes, then stir in the oregano and bouillon. Check the seasoning and add salt if needed (keep in mind that the bouillon already has salt).

5. Add the drained pasta to the skillet, mix well to completely coat the spaghetti with the sauce, and cook for 2 more minutes over low heat.

6. Serve on plates or in shallow bowls and garnish with the crema (about 1 tablespoon per plate), crumbled cheese, and parsley leaves.

NOTAS

✖ *If you can't find ripe and juicy tomatoes, use canned tomatoes instead.*

✖ *Instead of adding the crema as a garnish, some people like to mix it into the sauce at the end of step 4 to make a creamy Mexican spaghetti.*

MAIN DISHES

ESPAGUETI VERDE

Creamy Poblano Spaghetti

This green spaghetti is an excellent recipe for using poblano peppers, which add both flavor and color. The cream helps reduce any spiciness the poblanos may have. This spaghetti can be enjoyed on its own with a side salad or as a side dish for chicken, pork, or beef. Families also like preparing it during the holidays as an accompaniment to a baked turkey or a roasted pork leg.

PREP TIME: 20 minutes	**COOK TIME:** 20 minutes	**YIELD:** 4 servings

PASTA

1 teaspoon salt

8 ounces (227 g) uncooked spaghetti

SAUCE

2 large poblano peppers, roasted, seeds and veins removed, and cut into strips (see page 232 for roasting instructions)

⅓ white onion, chopped, or ½ teaspoon onion powder

1 large clove garlic, chopped, or ¼ teaspoon garlic powder

¼ cup (60 ml) whole milk

¾ cup (180 ml) heavy cream (see Notas)

1 tablespoon butter

Salt and black pepper

FOR GARNISHING

Flat-leaf parsley leaves

1. To make the pasta: Place 8 cups (2 quarts/1.9 L) of water in a medium pot and bring to a boil over medium-high heat. Once boiling, add the salt, then add the pasta. Once the water comes back to a boil, let the pasta cook for about 8 minutes for al dente pasta, then drain.

2. While the pasta is cooking, make the sauce: Place the poblano pepper strips, reserving some for garnishing, in a blender along with the onion, garlic, milk, and heavy cream and process until a smooth sauce.

3. In a large skillet, melt the butter over medium heat. Add the poblano cream sauce to the skillet and season with salt and pepper. Reduce the heat to medium-low and let the sauce gently simmer for 6 to 8 minutes, stirring frequently, until the sauce is hot and has a velvety consistency.

4. Add the drained pasta to the skillet, mix well to completely coat the spaghetti with the sauce, and let the pasta heat up again.

5. Serve on plates or in shallow bowls and garnish with parsley leaves and the reserved poblano pepper strips.

NOTAS

✳ *You can substitute the heavy cream with 6 ounces (170 g) of cream cheese to give the sauce a thicker and richer texture.*

✳ *Seasoning the sauce with chicken bouillon granules is common. Add 1 teaspoon after you add the sauce to the skillet in step 3, making sure to adjust the salt accordingly because the bouillon is salty.*

TORTITAS DE PAPA

Potato Patties

These potato patties are often cooked around Lent, but you can prepare them any time of year. Made with a mixture of potato and cheese, *tortitas de papa* are a scrumptious meatless meal that is loved by children. This recipe takes me back to my childhood, because my mom used to make these for my siblings and me. As part of her low-budget cooking, she often used potatoes in a variety of different dishes, and this was one of my absolute favorites. I like serving these patties with a side salad and a red salsa.

PREP TIME: 5 minutes	**COOK TIME:** 35 minutes	**YIELD:** 10 potato patties

1½ pounds (680 g) potatoes (about 2 large potatoes), skins on and left whole (see Notas)

1 cup (120 g) crumbled queso fresco or shredded queso panela (see Notas)

1 large egg, beaten

Salt and black pepper

½ cup (65 g) all-purpose flour

½ cup (120 ml) vegetable oil, divided

1. Place the potatoes in a large saucepan and cover with enough water so that the water level is 1 inch (2.5 cm) above the potatoes. Place over medium-high heat and bring to a boil. Once boiling, reduce the heat and let simmer for 20 to 25 minutes, until the potatoes are tender. The potatoes are ready when a knife can easily slip in and out of them. (Do not overcook the potatoes because they will have a gummy texture when mashed.) Drain the water from the saucepan. When the potatoes are cool enough to handle, remove their skins.

2. Place the potatoes in a large bowl and mash them with a potato masher until they are soft and slightly creamy. Do NOT add any liquid. Mix in the cheese and beaten egg (the mixture will be a little stiff, but this is okay). Season with salt and pepper, then mix well until you have a uniform mashed-potato mixture.

3. For the patties, form balls about 1¾ inches (4.5 cm) in diameter, then gently pat them down with your fingers to flatten them.

4. Spread the flour on a plate and dredge both sides of a patty in the flour to coat it, then transfer it to a tray while you finish coating the rest of the patties. Shake off any excess flour.

5. In a large skillet, heat ¼ cup (60 ml) of the oil over medium-high heat. Cook half of the potato patties, turning them occasionally, until they are golden brown, 5 to 6 minutes total. Drain the patties and transfer to a paper towel-lined plate to absorb any excess oil. Add the remaining ¼ cup (60 ml) oil, cook the remaining patties, and transfer to the plate.

6. Serve warm with salad and salsa.

NOTAS

* I prefer to use red or Yukon Gold potatoes.

* Cooking the potatoes with their peels on helps the potato mixture have the appropriate consistency; otherwise, they absorb too much water.

* You can also use queso Cotija or Parmesan. Just keep in mind that some cheeses are saltier than others

VEGGIE TAMALES

A majority of the *tamal* recipes in Mexico use pork lard to prepare the dough, so I was intrigued when a friend of mine sent me a recipe years ago that used vegetable oil instead of lard. After experimenting with oil, I decided to create a recipe that's not only vegetarian but also vegan! An added benefit of using vegetable oil is that it renders a remarkably smooth dough that is easier to spread on the corn husks when assembling the tamales. Since creating this recipe, I have been continuously surprised by how foolproof it is. It only yields twelve tamales, but you can easily multiply the ingredients to make a bigger batch.

PREP TIME: 20 minutes	**COOK TIME:** 1 hour and 15 minutes	**YIELD:** 12 tamales

12 large corn husks, plus 10 for lining the steamer pot

2½ cups (250 g) masa harina for tamales

½ teaspoon baking powder

2 teaspoons salt, plus more if needed

¼ teaspoon onion powder, plus more if needed

¼ teaspoon garlic powder, plus more if needed

2¼ cups (540 ml) warm water or vegetable broth

¾ cup (180 ml) vegetable oil (see Notas on page 150)

2 cups (255 g) finely chopped mixed vegetables (carrot, squash, poblano pepper, red pepper, and fresh corn kernels)

1. Place all the husks in a large pot filled with hot water to soften and make pliable, about 20 minutes. (You can place a heavy plate on top of the husks to keep them submerged inside the pot.)

2. While the husks soak, in a large bowl, thoroughly mix the masa harina with the baking powder, salt, onion powder, and garlic powder. Gradually add the warm water to the bowl and continue mixing until all the liquid is well incorporated.

3. Slowly pour the oil into the bowl, mixing it into the dough to form a creamy texture. Taste the dough and adjust the salt, garlic powder, and/or onion powder if needed. (Keep in mind that the dough will lose some of its saltiness during the steaming process.)

4. Remove the husks from the water, pat dry with a kitchen towel, and let air-dry. While the husks are drying, mix the chopped vegetables into the corn dough, stirring well.

5. To assemble the tamales, spread 6 tablespoons of the dough onto a corn husk. Fold the sides of the corn husk inward and then fold the narrow end part up toward the center of the tamal. Place the formed tamal on a tray while you assemble the remaining 11 tamales.

(continued)

6. To steam the tamales, place a steamer rack inside a large stockpot. Add enough warm water up to the level of the steamer rack, then line the rack with a layer of corn husks. Place the tamales in the pot in an upright position, with the open ends facing up. Cover them with a generous layer of husks, then cover the pot with the lid. Steam the tamales for 1 hour and 15 minutes over medium-high heat. During the steaming, check the pot to see if it has enough water (be careful when removing the lid), adding more if needed (see Notas). To check if the tamales are ready, remove one from the pot using kitchen tongs and let sit on a plate for 5 minutes. (This will give the dough a chance to solidify after coming out of the steaming pot.) After the waiting time, open the tamal. If the husk separates easily from the dough, that means the tamal is ready; if the dough sticks to the husk, place it back in the pot and cook for 15 more minutes.

7. Serve while they are still hot.

NOTAS

✳ *Use a neutral vegetable oil, such as canola, sunflower, peanut, corn, or even light olive oil.*

✳ *If you need to add more water to the pot when steaming the tamales, make sure to pour it as close to the side of the pot as possible, avoiding the tamales. If water gets into the tamales, they will lose their flavor and the dough will be soggy.*

✳ *Other types of vegetables to try are potatoes, chayotes, green peas, and sweet potatoes. Chopped leafy greens, such as Swiss chard or spinach, are good options as well and give the dough a green hue.*

✳ *If you want to boost the protein content, add cooked chickpeas with the vegetables.*

✳ *You can also add strips of cheese as a filling, such as queso fresco, panela, or Oaxaca, or even mozzarella.*

✳ *You can store the tamales in plastic bags in your freezer for up to 4 months. To reheat, allow the tamales to defrost, then place them in a steamer for 10 to 15 minutes. You can also pop them in the microwave on the high setting for about 1 minute.*

TAMALES DE HOJA DE PLÁTANO

Tamales Wrapped in Banana Leaves

I grew up eating these *tamales* because the recipe is from Veracruz, where my mother and grandmother are from, but you can also find them in parts of Tamaulipas, San Luis Potosí, and Puebla. In Mexico, the two most common wrappings for tamales are corn husks and banana leaves. Tamales wrapped in banana leaves are more popular in the south and on the two coasts, regions where the production of banana leaves is plentiful. It's easier to wrap tamales in banana leaves than corn husks, but the really special part of using banana leaves is the distinct flavor, color, and aroma they add to the dough. This recipe, from Veracruz, has a sauce made with dried peppers, but in other places, people might use a tomato-based, mole, or achiote sauce.

PREP TIME: 1 hour	**COOK TIME:** 1 hour and 45 minutes	**YIELD:** 12 large tamales

PORK

2 pounds (907 g) pork shoulder, cut into 1½-inch (4 cm) cubes

1 bay leaf

¼ small white onion

1 clove garlic

ADOBO SAUCE

3 ancho peppers, seeds and veins removed

3 guajillo peppers, seeds and veins removed

1 morita or chipotle pepper (optional)

1 Roma or plum tomato

¼ white onion, thickly sliced

2 cloves garlic, unpeeled

½ teaspoon black peppercorns

1 tablespoon masa harina

Salt

1. To make the pork: Place the meat, bay leaf, onion quarter, and garlic clove in a large pot and cover the ingredients with water. Bring to a boil over medium-high heat. Once boiling, reduce the heat to low and let simmer for about 30 minutes, or until the meat is cooked. (The meat does not need to be fork-tender because it will keep cooking when you steam the tamales.) Place the meat in a large bowl, reserving the cooking broth (which will be used to make the dough).

2. While the pork is cooking, make the adobo sauce: Heat a comal over low heat. Once hot, lightly toast the ancho, guajillo, and morita peppers. Gently press the peppers with a wooden spatula to make sure that they toast evenly. After a few seconds, as soon as the skin of the peppers start forming some blisters, remove them from the comal (do not let them burn). Place the toasted peppers in a large bowl and cover them with hot water. Let them soak for 20 minutes, or until soft. (You can place a heavy plate on top of the peppers to keep them submerged in the water.)

3. On the same comal, roast the tomato, onion slices, and 2 garlic cloves, rotating them to achieve an even roasting. Remove the garlic and onion promptly because they will take less time to roast. The tomato will take about 8 minutes to roast. After roasting the vegetables, toast the peppercorns for a few seconds, or until they start releasing their aroma. Remove from the heat and let cool.

(continued)

DOUGH

1¼ cups (360 g) lard

1 teaspoon salt

4 cups (400 g) masa harina for tortillas

4 large banana leaves, cut into 14 pieces (11-inch/28-cm squares) and prepped (see page 15)

(see page 15)

NOTAS

* *If you need to add more water to the pot when steaming the tamales, make sure to pour it as close to the side of the pot as possible, avoiding the tamales.*

* *This recipe only yields 12 tamales, so double or triple the recipe if you want to have some extra tamales in your freezer to enjoy later.*

* *You can omit the morita pepper, or add more if you like it spicy.*

* *You can store the tamales in plastic bags in your freezer for up to 4 months. To reheat, allow the tamales to defrost, then place them in a steamer for 10 to 15 minutes. You can also pop them in the microwave on the high setting for about 1 minute.*

4. Drain the soaked peppers, reserving 1 cup (240 ml) of the soaking water. Place the peppers in a blender along with the roasted tomato, onion, garlic (peeled), peppercorns, ½ cup (120 ml) of the pepper soaking water, and the 1 tablespoon masa harina. Process until a fine, thick sauce. Season the sauce with salt, add it to the bowl with the meat, and mix well. If the sauce is too dry, add a little bit more of the pepper soaking water.

5. To make the dough: Place the lard and salt in a large bowl. Beat the lard with an electric mixer (or by hand) until it is light and creamy. Slowly incorporate the 4 cups (450 g) masa harina and 3½ cups (840 ml) of the reserved pork broth, a little at a time, until the dough is well mixed, smooth, and homogenous with a creamy and spreadable consistency. Taste the dough and add more salt if needed. (Keep in mind that the dough will lose some of its saltiness during the steaming process.)

6. To assemble the tamales, place ¼ cup (60 g) of the dough onto a banana leaf piece. Using a spatula or the back of a spoon, spread the dough around to form a rough circle of 4½ to 5 inches (11 to 12.5 cm) in diameter. The thickness of this layer of dough should be about ¼ inch (6 mm) thick. Top the dough with 1 or 2 pieces of the meat and some of the adobo sauce. Fold both sides inward toward the center, then fold the bottom and top ends of the leaf toward the center. Place the wrapped tamal on a tray while you finish wrapping the remaining 11 tamales.

7. To steam the tamales, place a steamer rack inside a large stockpot. Add enough warm water up to the level of the steamer rack, then line the rack with 1 or 2 pieces of banana leaves. Place the tamales horizontally in the pot, layering all of them on top of each other in a staggered manner (like bricks on a wall). Cover the tamales with more banana leaf pieces, then cover the pot with the lid. (You can also cover the banana leaves with an added layer of aluminum foil to form a better seal.) Steam the tamales for 1 hour and 15 minutes over medium-high heat. During the steaming, check the pot to see if it has enough water (be careful when removing the lid), adding more if needed (see Notas). To check if the tamales are ready, remove one from the pot using kitchen tongs and let sit on a plate for 5 minutes. (This will give the dough a chance to solidify after coming out of the steaming pot.) After the waiting time, open the tamal. If the banana leaf separates easily from the dough when you open it, then the tamales are ready; if not, then return the tamal to the pot and continue cooking for 15 more minutes.

8. Serve while they are still hot.

SIDES, SALSAS & PEPPERS

MOROS CON CRISTIANOS

Black Beans and Rice

Black beans and rice, also known as *moros con Christianos* or *Casamiento*, is a popular side dish in the state of Veracruz, where it is sometimes served alongside Plátanos Fritos (page 174). Moros con Cristianos can also be found in some other parts of Mexico, as well as in the Caribbean and throughout Latin America (the dish originated in Cuba). My version adds a few more spices than the traditional recipe because I love how flavorful they make the dish (see Notas). This side is wonderful served alongside fried fish or roasted chicken, or just with a fried egg and guacamole on top. It can even make a great meatless meal.

PREP TIME: 5 minutes	**COOK TIME:** 15 minutes	**YIELD:** 6 servings

1 tablespoon vegetable oil or lard

¼ cup (35 g) finely chopped white onion

1 clove garlic, minced

1 cup (175 g) cooked or canned black beans

1½ cups (250 g) cooked long-grain white rice

¼ cup (60 ml) black bean cooking broth

Salt

½ teaspoon dried Mexican oregano

Pinch of ground cumin (optional)

1. In a large skillet, heat the oil or lard over medium-high heat. Add the onion and garlic and cook and stir until the onion is translucent, 2 to 3 minutes.

2. Add the beans to the pan and cook for about 2 more minutes, allowing them to absorb the flavors of the onion and garlic.

3. Stir in the rice, then add the bean broth. Cook for about 5 minutes, or until everything is hot.

4. Season with salt and add the oregano and cumin (if using), stir well, and serve.

NOTAS

* *This dish traditionally doesn't include oregano and cumin, but I find that adding these spices really enhances its flavor.*
* *Some cooks in Veracruz like to add their own touch to this dish, like stirring in some chopped serrano peppers or diced tomato while cooking the onion and garlic in step 1.*

FRIJOLES CHARROS

Charro Beans

Frijoles charros is a hearty and flavorful dish that is commonly used as a side dish for grilled meats in the northern states of Mexico. In that part of the country, it would be impossible to go to a *carne asada* and not find a pot of these beans on the table or over the fire. *Frijoles charros* means "charro beans," with *charro* being the name for traditional Mexican cowboys. Filled with a variety of cooked meats, this dish is emblematic of the north's love of grilling and makes a perfect addition to any barbecue or cookout, though they can be enjoyed by themselves.

PREP TIME: 15 minutes	**COOK TIME:** 20 minutes	**YIELD:** 8 servings

3½ ounces (100 g) Mexican chorizo

3½ ounces (100 g) chopped bacon

3½ ounces (100 g) chopped cooked ham

1½ cups pork cracklings (50 g) and/or chopped or sliced hot dog sausages (225 g) (optional)

¼ medium onion, finely chopped

2 cloves garlic, minced

2 serrano peppers, minced

2 large tomatoes, chopped (about 2½ cups/450 g)

6 cups (1 kg) cooked pinto beans with their broth, still in the cooking pot (see Notas for cooking instructions)

Salt

1 cup (40 g) finely chopped fresh cilantro

FOR SERVING

Warm corn or flour tortillas

1. Heat a large skillet over medium heat. Add the chorizo and bacon and cook and stir for about 10 minutes. Add the ham and pork cracklings (if using) and cook for about 5 minutes.

2. Add the onion, garlic, and peppers and cook and stir for 2 more minutes. Add the tomatoes and cook, stirring occasionally, for 8 minutes. Once the tomatoes have released their juices, transfer the mixture in the skillet to the pot with the beans and stir to combine everything. Let simmer for about 15 minutes over low heat to blend the flavors.

3. Season with salt and top with the cilantro right before serving.

4. Ladle the soup into bowls and serve with warm tortillas.

NOTAS

* *To cook the beans, place 2 cups (390 g) of dried pinto beans, ¼ of a medium white onion, 2 garlic cloves, and 8 cups (2 quarts/1.9 L) of water in a large pot. Cook, covered, over medium-high heat for about 2 hours, or until they are tender. You can also cook the beans in in an Instant Pot on the "Beans" setting in 30 minutes.*

* *Some people like to add beer to their frijoles charros.*

FRIJOLES PUERCOS

A scrumptious and crowd-pleasing dish, *frijoles puercos* is made with beans, chorizo, and melted cheese. Its name roughly translates to "porky beans." This recipe can be used as a side dish or as an appetizer when served with tortilla chips. Frijoles puercos originated in the state of Sinaloa, but it is also popular throughout the neighboring states of Sonora and Chihuahua. In that part of the country, you can find this dish served at barbecues, birthday parties, and weddings. If you want to make it for your next get-together, I recommend serving it alongside a bowl of guacamole, your favorite salsas, and a generous amount of tortilla chips.

PREP TIME: 10 minutes	**COOK TIME:** 20 minutes	**YIELD:** 4 servings

2 cups (12 ounces/350 g) cooked or canned pinto beans, plus ⅓ cup (80 g) of the bean cooking broth or liquid from the can

3 ounces (85 g) Mexican chorizo, casing removed

3 ounces (85 g) Muenster or Monterey Jack, shredded (see Notas)

1 tablespoon finely chopped pickled jalapeño peppers

1 tablespoon lard or butter (see Notas)

Salt

FOR SERVING

Tortilla chips

Warm flour tortillas

1. Add the beans and bean broth to a blender and process until a smooth paste.

2. Heat a large skillet over medium heat. Add the chorizo and cook for 6 to 8 minutes, using a spatula or a wooden spoon to crumble the chorizo into pieces while it is cooking. Stir the chorizo often so that it does not stick to the pan. Allow it to release its fat content.

3. Add the bean paste to the pan with the chorizo. Once the beans start releasing steam, add the cheese and jalapeños and keep stirring until the cheese begins to melt. Add the lard, season with salt, and reduce the heat to low. Keep stirring to prevent the cheese from sticking to the pan. Continue cooking and stirring for 3 minutes.

4. Serve the beans with tortilla chips and tortillas (see Notas).

NOTAS

* This dish is usually made using a melting cheese called Chihuahua, from the state with the same name, but you can use Muenster or Monterey Jack. In the state of Sonora, some cooks use a mix of American and Chihuahua cheeses.

* Frijoles puercos is traditionally made with lard, but you can use butter, oil, or margarine.

* You can adjust the amounts of cheese and lard to your liking.

* The beans will be very hot when they are done cooking, so you may want to let them cool a bit before eating them.

FRIJOLES COLADOS

Yucatán Fried Beans

Frijoles colados literally translates to "strained beans" and, as the name suggests, is a preparation of beans that renders a thin, silky texture. This is a typical way of preparing beans in the Yucatán Peninsula, where this dish is served as a side. You can also find frijoles colados used as a filling in tortas with Cochinita Pibil (page 113) and Pickled Red Onions (page 187). They are also used to make a traditional antojito called *panuchos*.

PREP TIME: 10 minutes	**COOK TIME:** 10 minutes	**YIELD:** 8 servings

2 thick slices large white onion

1 habanero pepper (see Notas)

4 cups (700 g) cooked black beans (see Notas)

1 cup (240 ml) black bean cooking broth

¼ cup lard (50 g) or vegetable oil (60 ml)

Salt

1. Heat a comal over medium heat. Roast the onion slices and the habanero pepper, occasionally turning them to avoid burning them and to make sure they are roasted evenly.

2. Chop the roasted onion and add it to a blender along with the beans and their cooking broth. Process until a smooth puree.

3. In a large skillet, heat the lard or oil over medium heat. Pour the bean puree through a fine-mesh strainer into the skillet. Cook for 2 minutes, stirring frequently, then reduce the heat to low.

4. Add the roasted habanero pepper to the beans and continue cooking for 4 to 5 minutes over low heat, stirring occasionally to keep the beans from sticking to the bottom of the skillet, until the beans have reached your preferred texture (dry, creamy, or more liquid. Serve immediately.

NOTAS

* *Leaving the roasted habanero pepper whole does not add spiciness to the beans; it only adds some of its distinct flavor to the dish. You can also use serrano pepper, although it will not have the same flavor.*

* *You can prepare this recipe using canned beans. Keep in mind that 1 can (15 ounces/425 g) renders about 2 cups of drained cooked beans, depending on the brand.*

* *Some cooks like to cook the onion slices and habanero pepper in the same lard that the beans will be cooked in. Sometimes they immediately discard the habanero after cooking it, letting it only infuse its flavor into the oil.*

QUESO FUNDIDO

Queso fundido is a fantastic appetizer that is popular in northern Mexico and often associated with grilling culture. It can be found at neighborhood *carne asadas* in the northern states, as well as in steakhouses all over the country. Translating to "molten cheese," queso fundido consists of melted cheese garnished with pieces of chorizo and is often served with tortillas or tortilla chips. Preparing queso fundido in an iron skillet or a cazuela gives it a special rustic touch and a delightful flavor. The melted cheese and savory chorizo create a scrumptious flavor combination that makes everyone's mouth water. You can make queso fundido in a variety of ways: You can bake it in the oven (like in this recipe), place it under the broiler, microwave it, or melt the cheese in a skillet and scoop it onto a plate. If you're using a grill, you can place a skillet right on the grill so that the cheese melts while you cook your steaks.

PREP TIME: 5 minutes	**COOK TIME:** 20 minutes	**YIELD:** 6 servings

1 tablespoon vegetable oil (optional; see Notas)

6 ounces (170 g) Mexican chorizo (about 2 medium-size chorizo links), casings removed (see Notas)

12 ounces (340 g) queso Oaxaca or Monterey Jack or Muenster cheese, shredded

FOR SERVING

1½ cups roasted salsa

6 medium-size flour tortillas or 12 ounces (340 g) tortilla chips

NOTAS

✗ *If your chorizo has enough fat you may not need to use the vegetable oil.*

✗ *If you choose to make queso fundido on the stove, grill, or even in the microwave, be sure to stir the cheese frequently so that it melts evenly.*

1. Preheat the oven to 350°F (175°C). In a large skillet, heat the oil (if using). Add the chorizo to the skillet and cook for 6 to 7 minutes, stirring frequently to cook evenly and to keep it from sticking to the bottom. Once the chorizo is cooked, remove any excess fat from the skillet, or place the cooked chorizo on a paper towel–lined plate to absorb the excess fat.

2. Set aside 2 tablespoons of cooked chorizo to use for garnish. Equally divide the rest of the cooked chorizo between two small oven-safe dishes (4 to 5 inches/10 to 12.5 cm in length or diameter) or place into one large oven-safe dish (8 to 10 inches/20 to 25 cm in length or diameter) in an even layer. Evenly spread the cheese over the chorizo.

3. Bake for 10 to 12 minutes, until the cheese is melted and bubbling. (Be careful not to overcook it, as it may result in a chewy texture.)

4. Place the dish(es) on a heatproof surface. Garnish with the reserved cooked chorizo and serve warm with the salsa and flour tortillas or tortilla chips for dipping.

CALABACITAS CON ELOTE

Mexican-Style Corn and Zucchini

Calabacitas con elote, which translates to "zucchini with corn," is a simple but useful recipe to have in your repertoire. It can serve as a side dish for many stews and dishes, but you can also enjoy it as a stand-alone meal. In this case, I like to serve it with corn tortillas and black beans from the pot. This makes for a colorful and delicious vegetarian meal.

PREP TIME: 10 minutes	**COOK TIME:** 20 minutes	**YIELD:** 6 servings

2 tablespoons vegetable or canola oil

½ cup (55 g) finely chopped white onion

1 clove garlic, minced

2 medium zucchini, diced (about 3 cups/345 g)

2 serrano peppers, finely chopped

2½ cups (365 g) fresh corn kernels (see Nota)

3 cups (540 g) diced tomatoes (about 3 medium tomatoes)

Salt and black pepper

FOR GARNISHING AND SERVING

2 tablespoons chopped fresh cilantro

Black beans from the pot

Warm corn tortillas or white or red rice

1. In a large skillet, heat the oil over medium-high heat. Add the onion and garlic and cook and stir until the onion starts to turn translucent, 2 to 3 minutes. Add the zucchini and serrano peppers and cook, stirring occasionally, for 5 more minutes.

2. Add the corn and cook for 3 minutes, stirring frequently to prevent browning. Add the tomatoes, stir, and season with salt and black pepper.

3. Cover the skillet with the lid, reduce the heat to low, and let simmer until the zucchini and corn are tender, 8 to 10 minutes.

4. Garnish with the cilantro and serve with black beans and corn tortillas or rice.

NOTA *You can use frozen corn to make this recipe during the winter.*

PAPAS CON RAJAS Y CREMA

Creamy Poblano Potatoes

This is an easy vegetarian recipe that can be a side dish or a light meal. It consists of poblano pepper strips and diced potatoes in a rich cream sauce. It is similar to the common Mexican dish *rajas con crema* (poblano strips with cream) but uses potatoes. This dish is an excellent accompaniment to grilled chicken, steak, or even fish. Besides serving it as a side, you can also use these potatoes as a vegetarian taco filling with corn tortillas.

PREP TIME: 10 minutes	**COOK TIME:** 20 minutes	**YIELD:** 4 servings

1 pound (454 g) golden, red, or white potatoes (see Notas), peeled and cut into 1-inch (2.5 cm) cubes

2 tablespoons vegetable oil

½ medium white onion, sliced ¼ inch thick (6 mm)

2 poblano peppers, roasted, seeds and veins removed, and cut into strips (see page 232 for roasting instructions)

½ cup (120 ml) Mexican crema

Salt and black pepper

1. Place the potatoes in a medium saucepan and cover with water. Cook over medium-high heat until they are cooked but still firm, about 15 minutes (see Notas). (Make sure to check the potatoes occasionally so that they don't overcook). Drain.

2. While the potatoes are cooking, in a large skillet, heat the oil over medium-high heat. Add the onion and cook until translucent, about 3 minutes (see Notas).

3. Add the drained potatoes and cook for 3 minutes, then stir in the roasted pepper strips and pour in the crema. Season with salt and pepper. Keep cooking for 2 to 3 minutes to warm the peppers and the crema. Serve warm.

NOTAS

✳ *Do not use russet potatoes for this recipe, as they tend to break apart easily.*

✳ *The cooking time for this recipe will vary depending on the variety of potatoes you use. Just make sure the potatoes are cooked but still hold their shape.*

✳ *I like cooking the onion slices a little bit longer, until they start turning golden around the edges, to give them a little more flavor.*

✳ *If you like spicy food, add 1 jalapeño pepper, cut into thin slices, in step 2 with the onion.*

ENSALADA DE NOPALES

Cactus Paddle Salad

The nopal cactus, native to Mexico, has been an integral part of the country's cuisine for centuries. To prepare for consumption, the paddles are cut from the cactus plant and then cleaned and removed of their spines. These paddles are what we refer to as *nopales* in Mexican cooking, and they have been a hearty and staple ingredient since the time of the Aztecs. They are often cut into small pieces and cooked in stews, mixed with eggs (page 31), blended in green smoothies and juices (page 224), and used in side dishes and salads, like this *ensalada de nopales*. Also called *nopalitos compuestos*, this salad is one of the most popular ways to enjoy nopales. Here, I have included general instructions for cooking nopales for lots of dishes.

PREP TIME: 10 minutes	**COOK TIME:** 10 minutes	**YIELD:** 4 servings

NOPALES

6 nopales, cleaned and chopped (see page 11 for nopales prep)

¼ white onion

1 clove garlic

½ teaspoon salt

NOPALES SALAD

1½ cups (270 g) diced tomato

2 serrano peppers, finely chopped

½ cup (55 g) finely chopped onion

½ cup (20 g) chopped fresh cilantro

⅓ cup (80 ml) olive oil

2 tablespoons fresh lemon juice

1 teaspoon dried Mexican oregano

Salt and black pepper

FOR GARNISHING AND SERVING

½ cup (60 g) crumbled queso fresco

Thinly sliced radish (optional)

Sliced serrano pepper (optional)

1 avocado, sliced

Corn tostadas

1. To cook the nopales (see Notas): Fill a medium pot with 4 quarts (3.8 L) of water and bring to a boil over medium-high heat. Once boiling, add the nopales, onion quarter, garlic clove, and salt. Reduce the heat to low and let simmer for 8 to 10 minutes, until the nopales turn a pale-green color. The nopales will exude a sticky substance (see Notas), and often a foam, so pay attention to avoid having the foam spill over. Drain the nopales completely. Some people like to rinse the nopales to remove any extra sticky substance. I used to do that but then realized that this step takes away some of their flavor. (Now your nopales are ready to be used in salads, scrambled eggs, Mexican stews, etc.)

2. To make the nopales salad: Place the cooked nopales in a large bowl. Add the tomato, serrano peppers, chopped onion, and cilantro and gently mix everything together.

3. In a small bowl, mix the olive oil, lemon juice, oregano, and salt and black pepper until well combined. Drizzle the dressing into the bowl with the nopales and lightly toss so that everything is well coated.

4. Garnish the salad with queso fresco and radish and pepper slices (if using) and serve with avocado and corn tostadas.

NOTAS

✶ *People have different techniques for reducing the slimy texture that forms while cooking nopales, including cooking them in a copper cauldron, using green tomatillo husks, or adding a tablespoon of baking soda to the water before cooking. To use the tomatillo method, add the husk of 1 tomatillo to the cooking water of the nopales in step 1 and discard it once the nopales are cooked.*

✶ *To preserve the crispness of nopales, avoid overcooking them (e.g., if they are being added to a stew, they will continue to cook for a few more minutes in the stew).*

✶ *Precooked nopales can be added to dishes and stews in the same way you would add carrots or green beans.*

HONGOS SALTEADOS

Sautéed Mushrooms

Sautéed mushrooms are a popular filling for quesadillas and empanadas in Mexico City and the surrounding central area of Mexico. These mushrooms are quick and easy to make and can be a side dish for any meal or a filling for tacos, quesadillas, gorditas, and more.

PREP TIME: 10 minutes	**COOK TIME:** 10 minutes	**YIELD:** 4 servings

1 tablespoon olive oil

1 tablespoon salted butter

2 green onions (see Notas), finely chopped

1 clove garlic, minced

1 guajillo pepper, seeds and veins removed and sliced into rings

2 árbol peppers (see Notas), finely chopped

10 ounces white, cremini, or portobello mushrooms, chopped

2 to 4 fresh epazote leaves, chopped (see Notas)

Salt and black pepper

1. In a large skillet, heat the oil and butter over medium heat. Add the green onions and garlic and cook and stir until the green onions look a little soft, making sure the garlic does not burn.

2. Add the guajillo and árbol peppers and mushrooms and toss to stir. Cook for 4 to 5 minutes, stirring occasionally, until the mushrooms are slightly golden brown and have shrunk a little bit in size.

3. Remove the pan from the heat (see Notas), stir in the epazote, and season with salt and black pepper.

4. Serve warm.

NOTAS

✱ *You can substitute the green onions with ½ cup (55 g) of finely chopped white onion.*

✱ *This dish is traditionally cooked only with the guajillo pepper, but I add the árbol peppers for some heat. You can omit the árbol peppers if you do not want the dish to be spicy.*

✱ *If you can only find dried epazote, use 1 teaspoon. Fresh cilantro is a good substitute, although it does not have the same flavor profile as epazote.*

✱ *I usually remove the skillet quickly from the heat to keep the mushrooms plump and juicy.*

✱ *To make a classic mushroom quesadilla, warm a freshly made corn tortilla over a hot comal and add a generous amount of Oaxaca cheese or any other melting cheese. Fill the center with a portion of these mushrooms and fold. Continue cooking, turning the quesadilla over once, until the cheese is melted to your liking. You can also place a whole epazote leaf inside the quesadilla to give it an aromatic touch.*

PLÁTANOS FRITOS
Fried Plantains

I worked as a teacher for several years in the southern state of Tabasco, and part of my time there was spent in an area known as La Chontalpa. It is a place filled with abundant vegetation, and green year-round. Its two main crops are cocoa beans and different types of bananas and plantains. Fried plantains are the most common way to eat plantains in all the regions of Mexico that consume them. They are great as a side dish for a Mexican brunch, served alongside rice, refried black beans, and enchiladas or entomatadas. Alternatively, they can be enjoyed alone as a dessert.

PREP TIME: 5 minutes	**COOK TIME:** 20 minutes	**YIELD:** 4 servings

2 large plantains, ripe but still firm

⅓ cup (80 ml) vegetable oil

TOPPINGS (OPTIONAL)

¼ cup (60 ml) Mexicana crema or sour cream

¼ cup (30 g) crumbled queso fresco or panela (see Notas)

2 tablespoons butter

¼ cup (60 ml) sweetened condensed mllk

1. Cut off the tips of the plantains with a sharp knife, then make a slit along each plantain from top to bottom to open and remove the peel. Slice the plantains diagonally into ½-inch-thick (13 mm) pieces, or slice in half lengthwise (a firmer plantain will be easier to hold when slicing). You can also leave them whole (see Notas).

2. In a large skillet, heat the oil over medium-high heat. Wait until the oil is hot, but not smoking, then add the plantain slices, cooking in batches. Cook the slices for 4 to 5 minutes on each side, until golden brown, then use a slotted spoon to transfer them to a paper towel–lined plate to absorb any excess oil. (They will be extremely hot, so be careful and let them cool for a few minutes before eating.)

3. Serve the plantains on a plate with the toppings of your choice.

NOTAS

✻ *You can substitute the queso fresco with feta or another crumbled cheese.*

✻ *Some people like frying the plantains whole. To do this, fry the whole plantains in the hot oil over medium-low heat, gently turning them to make sure that every side is cooked completely, 15 to 18 minutes, then transfer them to a paper towel–lined plate. To serve, cut them in half lengthwise and add the toppings of your choice.*

✻ *My grandma used to cook whole plantains in her wooden stove at her ranch. Sometimes, during the winter months when we light our fireplace, I like to place some plantains (wrapped in aluminum foil) near the fire logs to cook them, just like her. You can also do this on a grill.*

SALSA DE CHILE SERRANO
Fried Serrano Pepper Salsa

This green, spicy salsa is inspired by a popular table salsa found in my hometown of Tampico. It can also be found in the surrounding regions of the states of Veracruz and San Luis Potosí, in neighborhood restaurants and mom-and-pop diners. It is traditionally prepared by first frying the peppers whole to give them extra flavor, but the peppers are prone to bursting and even flying out of the pan if you fry them for too long, so I made some modifications to this recipe to make it easier to prepare.

PREP TIME: 5 minutes	**COOK TIME:** 10 minutes	**YIELD:** about 1 cup (240 ml)

1 cup (105 g) chopped serrano peppers

2 tablespoons vegetable oil

⅓ cup (40 g) finely chopped white onion

Salt

1. Place the serrano peppers in a blender with ½ cup (120 ml) of water. Process for a few seconds until a semi-coarse texture (if you over-blend to a finer texture, the salsa will still be okay).

2. In a medium skillet, heat the oil over medium-high heat. Add the onion and cook and stir until it starts to become transparent, about 2 minutes. Pour the pepper mixture into the pan. Once boiling, reduce the heat to low, cover with the lid, and cook for about 8 minutes. (If the liquid reduces while cooking, add a few tablespoons of water.) The salsa is ready when the peppers change from a bright green to a pale green and the oil floats to the surface.

3. Season the salsa with salt and serve at room temperature. Store in the refrigerator in an airtight container for up to 1 week.

NOTA
You can use the same process to make salsa using other peppers, such as jalapeño or bird.

ADOBO SAUCE

This adobo sauce is the same sauce found in several Mexican dishes, including Chilorio (page 48), enchiladas rojas, asado de puerco, tamales de puerco, and more. It is also used to make Birria de Res (page 95), Chorizo (page 122), and pozole rojo. Once you know how to make this sauce, you will be able to easily prepare all those classic dishes.

PREP TIME: 10 minutes plus 20 minutes soaking time	**YIELD:** 2 cups (480 ml)

4 guajillo peppers, seeds and veins removed

3 ancho peppers, seeds and veins removed

3 cups (720 ml) warm water

2 large cloves garlic, roughly chopped

¼ teaspoon black pepper

Salt

1. Place the guajillo and ancho peppers in a large bowl with the warm water and soak for 20 minutes, until soft. Reserve the soaking water. Transfer the soaked peppers to a blender along with the garlic, black pepper, and 1½ cups (360 ml) of the soaking water and process until a smooth and silky sauce (you do not want to have large pieces of pepper skins in it).

2. Pour the adobo sauce into a medium saucepan through a fine-mesh sieve. Season with salt and stir well (see Nota). Turn the heat to medium-high and bring to a boil. Once boiling, reduce the heat to low and let simmer for 8 to 10 minutes; the sauce will change from a deep red to a brownish red. Remove the saucepan from the heat.

3. Pour the sauce into a sterilized glass jar, tightly screw on the lid, and let cool completely before storing in the refrigerator for up to 3 days or in the freezer for 3 to 4 months (stir well after defrosting). When using the sauce to make a dish, season it according to the recipe that you are preparing.

> **NOTA** *To preserve the adobo sauce for a longer period of time, add 2 tablespoons of white vinegar in step 2 (before the sauce comes to a boil).*

SALSA PICANTE EMBOTELLADA

Bottled Red Hot Sauce

In Mexico, we love to add bottled hot sauce (*salsa*) to many things, including popcorn, potato chips, steamed corn on the cob, fruit, and countless other foods. We sometimes also add it to crispy tacos and tortas. For years, I have craved the salsa that was added to the tortas that an old man used to sell at the corner stand near my middle school. After a lot of experimentation, I came up with this recipe, which is my favorite re-creation of that sauce.

PREP TIME: 10 minutes	**COOK TIME:** 20 minutes	**YIELD:** 12 ounces (355 ml)

20 árbol peppers (see Notas), seeds removed

3 guajillo peppers (see Notas), seeds and veins removed

2 cloves garlic

⅓ cup (80 ml) white vinegar

1 teaspoon dried Mexican oregano

½ teaspoon ground cumin

½ teaspoon dried thyme (see Notas)

½ teaspoon dried marjoram (see Notas)

1 whole clove

6 peppercorns

Salt

NOTAS

* *You can adjust the spiciness of the sauce by changing the pepper amounts. Árbol peppers are hot, and guajillo peppers are mild.*

* *If you don't have the thyme and marjoram, you can eliminate them.*

* *Although you can use this sauce immediately, the flavors will be even better in 2 weeks.*

1. Place the árbol peppers, guajillo peppers, and garlic cloves in a medium saucepan and add 3 cups (720 ml) of water. Turn the heat to medium-high and bring to a boil. Once boiling, reduce the heat to a gentle simmer for about 20 minutes, or until the peppers are very soft. (Due to the fumes the peppers will give off, make sure that your kitchen windows are open and/or that your exhaust fan is on.)

2. Remove the saucepan from the heat and let the ingredients come to room temperature. Drain the saucepan, reserving 1 cup (240 ml) of the cooking water.

3. Once everything has cooled, place the peppers, garlic, vinegar, oregano, cumin, thyme, marjoram, clove, and peppercorns along with the reserved cooking water into a blender. Process until a very fine texture.

4. Pour the mixture through a fine-mesh strainer into the saucepan (the strainer will help remove any remaining pieces of pepper skins). Turn the heat to medium-high and let simmer for about 5 minutes; this is just enough time to reduce the salsa to a thicker consistency and allow the flavors of the spices to blend together. (Again, do not forget to have the windows open and/or the exhaust fan on.)

5. Remove the sauce from the heat and let cool. Pour the sauce into a sterilized bottle and secure with an airtight cap, lid, or cork (see Notas). Store in the refrigerator for up to 6 months.

COOKING WITH MOLE PASTE

Many home cooks in Mexico prepare *mole poblano* using store-bought mole paste. It's a convenient option that is easy to prepare and saves a lot of time. Even though the instructions on the packaging for mole paste only call for diluting it with chicken broth, it is common to add extra ingredients to make the mole to one's liking and to emulate a mole sauce made from scratch. Besides using mole sauce with chicken and rice, you can also use it to make Enmoladas (page 97).

PREP TIME: 10 minutes	**COOK TIME:** 20 minutes	**YIELD:** 8 servings

5 ounces (142 g) plum tomatoes (about 2 small tomatoes)

2 thick slices medium white onion

1 small clove garlic

1 corn tortilla (see Notas)

¼ teaspoon ground cinnamon

¼ teaspoon ground anise seed

1 jar mole paste (8¼ ounces/234 g)

4 to 5 cups (960 ml to 1.2 L) chicken broth, divided

½ tablet (1⅝ ounces/46 g) Mexican chocolate (see Notas)

Salt

1. Place the tomatoes, onion slices, and garlic clove in a medium saucepan. Cover with water and bring to a rolling boil over medium-high heat. Reduce the heat to low and cook for 8 minutes, or until the tomatoes are cooked. Drain the water from the pan.

2. Toast the tortilla on a hot comal until crispy and lightly browned. Place the tomatoes, onion, garlic, cinnamon, anise seed, and toasted tortilla in a blender. Process until a fine sauce.

3. Place the same saucepan over low heat and add the mole paste. Add 1 cup (240 ml) of the broth to the saucepan and stir to start diluting the paste. Add another cup (240 ml) of the broth along with the tomato sauce and chocolate. Stir well until the mole paste is completely diluted in the broth and the chocolate has completely dissolved, 8 to 10 minutes. The paste will get thicker as it keeps cooking, so add more broth as needed to achieve the desired thickness (traditional mole has the consistency of a thick gravy).

4. The mole sauce is now ready to use. If you are making mole sauce to serve with chicken, see Notas for instructions.

NOTAS

* If you don't have a tortilla, you can substitute it with 1 slice of toasted bread or 4 saltine crackers.

* If you like your mole to be on the sweeter side, add one more quarter of a chocolate tablet to your sauce.

* Mole paste is not traditionally spicy, but if you like to spice things up, add 1 chipotle pepper in adobo sauce (from a can). Rinse it beforehand to remove the vinegar flavor, then add it to the blender in step 3.

* To serve the mole sauce with chicken, add 8 cooked chicken pieces (about 1 whole chicken) to the sauce, season with salt, and gently simmer for about 5 minutes. Place a piece of chicken on a plate, cover with mole sauce, and sprinkle with some toasted sesame seeds. Serve with rice and warm corn tortillas.

CHILES TOREADOS

Seasoned Sautéed Peppers

Chiles toreados are peppers that are lightly sautéed and usually seasoned with soy sauce and lime. Commonly offered at Mexican restaurants, it's a great thing to order when you want a little something spicy to accompany your meal, and the salsas just aren't cutting it. Chiles toreados are easy to make at home and great to serve alongside tacos or grilled meats. You can make this dish with jalapeño or serrano peppers. To eat them, you can cut them into bite-size pieces with a fork and knife, but I like to simply grab them by the stem and take a bite in between mouthfuls of my food.

PREP TIME: 5 minutes	**COOK TIME:** 5 minutes	**YIELD:** 4 servings

6 to 8 serrano peppers or 4 jalapeño peppers

1 tablespoon vegetable oil

1 tablespoon fresh lime juice

Salt

2 teaspoons soy sauce (optional; see Notas)

1. Using your hand or a spoon, gently massage the peppers by rolling them back and forth; this will release the flavor and heat from their seeds and veins. Using the tip of a sharp knife, make a tiny incision in the peppers to keep them from bursting while cooking.

2. In a medium skillet, heat the oil over medium heat. Add the peppers and cook, turning frequently, for 4 to 5 minutes, until they form light-golden blisters on their skins. (Do not let them burn because they will develop a bitter taste.)

3. Transfer the peppers to a serving bowl, then add the lime juice and season with salt. If using the soy sauce, mix it with the lime juice before adding to the peppers (avoid adding salt in this case, because the soy sauce is already salty).

4. Serve warm or at room temperature.

NOTAS

* *Not everyone adds soy sauce to their chiles toreados, but it does add another note of flavor to the peppers.*

* *Some restaurants also sauté some spring onions with the peppers and serve them together. If you want to make it this way, add 6 spring onions to the skillet with the peppers in step 2 and cook them until their skins have a light-golden color.*

PICKLED JALAPEÑO PEPPERS AND CARROTS

Pickled jalapeño peppers and carrots are a staple in Mexican households. You can go into almost any kitchen and find a jar of them in the fridge or a can of them in the pantry. Mexicans use these peppers when eating a wide array of foods, including tortas, tacos, antojitos, roasted chicken, grilled meats, and even some salads, such as ensalada de pollo. As a result, these pickled peppers are a common sight in Mexican daily life. Most people buy their pickled jalapeños at the store, but you can also easily prepare them at home. This recipe renders a large amount, but if you want to make less, simply divide the ingredients to make a smaller batch. Other types of peppers that are commonly pickled in Mexico are serrano peppers and (to a lesser extent) habanero peppers. You can use the same process in this recipe to pickle almost any pepper you want.

PREP TIME: 10 minutes	**COOK TIME:** 15 minutes	**YIELD:** 4 pints (64 ounces/1.8 kg)

2 tablespoons olive oil

2 cups (240 g) peeled and sliced carrots (see Notas)

2 pounds (907 g) jalapeño peppers, sliced lengthwise or cut into rings (see Notas)

12 cloves garlic

1 large white onion, sliced

4 cups (1 quart/950 ml) white vinegar

4 bay leaves

1½ teaspoons dried thyme (see Notas)

1½ teaspoons dried marjoram (see Notas)

1 teaspoon dried Mexican oregano

1 teaspoon black peppercorns

1 teaspoon allspice berries

Salt

1. In a large nonaluminum pot, heat the olive oil over medium-high heat. Add the sliced carrots and cook for 4 to 5 minutes, stirring frequently; their color will change to a bright orange. (Do not overcook the carrots because they need to retain some crunchiness.)

2. Add the jalapeños, garlic, and onion to the pot. Cook for another 3 minutes, stirring frequently.

3. Add the vinegar, 1 cup (240 ml) of water, bay leaves, thyme, marjoram, oregano, peppercorns, allspice, and salt. Bring to a boil, then reduce the heat to low and let gently simmer for 5 minutes. Remove the pot from the heat and let the ingredients cool for a few minutes.

4. Divide the contents of the pot (both the vegetables and the liquid) evenly among four sterilized pint-size (16 ounces/454 g) glass canning jars with lids. Tightly screw on the lids and let the jars completely cool before storing in a cool, dry place, like a pantry.

5. These pickled peppers can be consumed immediately after they cool. If you use canning jars and their special lids, they can be stored for 9 to 12 months in a pantry or cupboard. Once you open a jar, store it in the refrigerator for 2 to 3 months and close the lid tightly after every use.

NOTAS

✱ *You can slice the carrots in rounds or diagonal slices, as long as they have a uniform thickness so that they all cook evenly.*

✱ *You can pickle the peppers whole, without slicing them. You will need to make a small incision in them to keep them from bursting during the cooking process.*

✱ *If you prefer to use fresh herbs, substitute the dried thyme with 4 sprigs of fresh thyme and the dried marjoram with 2 sprigs of fresh marjoram.*

✱ *Other vegetables you can add to this pickle, along with the carrots, are cauliflower florets, small whole mushrooms, and squash cut into ⅓-inch (8.5 mm) rounds. Add these vegetables in step 2. These pickles are great served as an appetizer.*

PICKLED WHITE ONION WITH HABANERO PEPPER

This quick pickle is a popular condiment in the southeast region of Mexico, particularly in the Yucatán Peninsula. There, you will find people making it with either white or red onions and serving it on their kitchen tables during the main meal of the day. It is also offered at local taquerias and small eateries. On top of being easy to make, this pickled onion is an excellent way to enhance the flavors of grilled meats, seafood, tacos, and more. It also pairs well with Cochinita Pibil (page 113), another recipe from the south of Mexico.

PREP TIME: 5 minutes plus 30 minutes chilling time	**YIELD:** 1 cup (240 ml)

1 large white onion, finely chopped

1 habanero pepper (see Notas), finely chopped

¼ cup (60 ml) fresh lime juice (see Notas)

Salt

1. In a medium bowl, combine the onion, habanero pepper, and lime juice and season with salt. Mix well, cover the bowl, and refrigerate for at least 30 minutes.

2. Use immediately or store in the refrigerator in a glass jar with a lid for up to 3 days.

NOTAS

× If you like it spicier, add an extra habanero to the mix. You can also use other peppers, such as serrano or jalapeño.

× Traditionally, bitter orange juice is used for this, but lime juice is a common substitute when it's unavailable.

PICKLED RED ONIONS

Growing up in the northern city of Tampico, I was only used to seeing white onion in the dishes of my hometown. This was until 1980, then I moved to the far south of Mexico for a teaching job, and my outlook on Mexican cooking took an unexpected (but delicious) turn when I was introduced to red onions. These vibrant red onions are an integral part of the cuisines found in the state of Yucatán and the surrounding states within the Yucatán Peninsula. One can hardly enjoy a traditional meal from this region without a side of pickled onions, which are commonly served on the table alongside stews and other local dishes. These pickled onions are almost always found on the table when eating Cochinita Pibil (page 113) or any other achiote-based dish. You can also use them to top certain tacos, tostadas, sandwiches, and even grilled meats.

PREP TIME: 10 minutes	**YIELD:** 1½ cups (175 g)

1 large red onion or 2 medium red onions, sliced ¼ inch (6 mm) thick

1 bay leaf

4 black peppercorns

½ teaspoon dried Mexican oregano

Salt

1 cup (240 ml) white vinegar

1. Place the onion slices in a large glass bowl or jar. Add the bay leaf, peppercorns, and oregano. Season with salt and mix well.
2. Pour the vinegar into the bowl or jar and cover. Refrigerate for a couple of hours before serving (although they will taste better after 1 day). Store in the refrigerator in a glass jar with a lid for up to 2 weeks.

NOTAS

- *Some cooks like to blanch the onions before pickling to mellow their taste.*
- *Sometimes I add a couple of allspice berries in step 1.*

DESSERTS & BREADS

POLVORONES SEVILLANOS

One of the many *polvorones* that you can find in Mexican bakeries, *polvorones Sevillanos* are traditional cookies that melt in your mouth. As the name suggests, this recipe originated in Spain, where a different version of this cookie is made—the Spanish version is thicker and has nuts. What's great about this recipe is how simple and foolproof it is. It only has three ingredients and is ready in a matter of minutes. These cookies are an excellent treat to bake for your family during the winter months, although in Mexico, they are enjoyed year-round. They are a great option for enjoying with your evening *cafecito*.

PREP TIME: 15 minutes	**COOK TIME:** 15 minutes	**YIELD:** 24 polvorones

1¾ cups plus 2 tablespoons (360 g) shortening, plus more for greasing

2 cups (260 g) all-purpose flour, plus more for dusting

3¼ cups (405 g) confectioners' sugar (see Notas), plus more for dusting

FOR SERVING

Coffee or milk

NOTAS

* *If you do not have confectioners' sugar, you can make your own using granulated sugar. Place it in a blender and pulverize it on the high setting.*

* *These cookies will keep well for 1 week in an airtight container at room temperature.*

1. Preheat the oven to 350°F (175°C) and grease two baking sheets with shortening (or line them with parchment paper).

2. In a large bowl, combine the flour and sugar and mix well. Add the shortening and mix it with your hands to form a dough. The texture of the dough will resemble big clumps at first, but once you keep mixing it and working it with your hands, it will begin to stick together (yet still be very easy to crumble). Divide the dough in half.

3. Place one of the dough halves on a floured work surface. Sprinkle a rolling pin with flour and roll out the dough until it is ⅜ inch (1 cm) thick. (You need to make sure that the dough does not stick to your work surface, so add more flour if needed.) Using a 3-inch (7.5 cm) round cookie cutter, cut out circles and place them spaced apart on one of the prepared baking sheets. Repeat this step with the other dough half.

4. Bake for 12 to 15 minutes, until the bottoms are light golden and the cookies are firm. Let cool completely, then use a small sieve to dust them with confectioners' sugar.

5. Serve with coffee or milk.

PAY DE PIÑA

Pineapple Pie

The tradition of eating something sweet with afternoon coffee is deeply rooted in Mexican culture. Even though many people are acquainted with Mexican sweet breads, such as Conchas (page 206), Mantecadas (page 205), and Polvorones Sevillanos (page 191), not everyone knows that we also make cakes and pies. This pineapple pie is another recipe inspired by my hometown of Tampico, where it is sold whole or in slices at bakeries all over town. Pineapples are cultivated nearby, so that might be why it became a popular pie filling.

PREP TIME: 15 minutes plus 30 minutes cooling time	**COOK TIME:** 1 hour and 10 minutes	**YIELD:** 8 servings

PIECRUST (SEE NOTAS)

2½ cups (325 g) all-purpose flour, plus more for dusting

⅓ cup (65 g) sugar

Pinch of salt

¾ cup (1½ sticks/170 g) cold unsalted butter, cut into small cubes

3 large eggs

1 or 2 tablespoons cold whole milk (optional)

1 egg yolk, beaten

FILLING

5 cups (825 g) cubed fresh pineapple (about 1 large pineapple)

1 cup (200 g) sugar (see Notas)

1 stick Mexican cinnamon (about 2½ inches/6 cm long)

5 tablespoons cornstarch

1. To make the piecrust: In a large bowl, combine the flour, the ⅓ cup (65 g) sugar, and the salt and mix well. Add the butter and, using a fork or pastry blender, mix until the texture resembles coarse cornmeal. Add the eggs, one at a time, and continue mixing with the fork or a pastry blender.

2. Place the dough on a work surface lightly dusted with flour and gently knead it with your hands to bring the dough together. If the dough is very dry, add the cold milk, 1 tablespoon at a time, to form a smooth dough.

3. Divide the dough in half, then press down on each piece to form a disc. Wrap each disc with plastic wrap and refrigerate for at least 30 minutes. Remove from the fridge when ready to bake and the filling has completely cooled.

4. Meanwhile, make the filling: Place the pineapple, the 1 cup (200 g) sugar, and the cinnamon stick in a large pot over low heat. In a small bowl, mix the cornstarch with 1 cup (240 ml) of water until the cornstarch completely dissolves. Pour the mixture into the pot and stir. Continue cooking the pineapple mixture for about 10 minutes, after which it will begin to thicken like a gruel. Once it thickens and becomes more transparent in color, cook for 5 more minutes, then remove from the heat and let cool completely before adding to the piecrust. Remove and discard the cinnamon stick.

5. To assemble the pie: Preheat the oven to 350°F (175°C). Using a floured rolling pin, roll out the dough on a lightly floured work surface to form two 12-inch (30 cm) circles that are about ¼ inch (6 mm) thick. Line a pie dish with one of the dough circles, then evenly pour the cooled pineapple filling over it. Place the other dough circle on top of the filling and cut a small vent in the center. Trim the excess dough from the edges and press down to form a seal between the top and bottom halves. Crimp the edges of the dough with your fingers, then brush the top crust with the beaten egg yolk.

6. Bake for 50 to 60 minutes, until the crust is golden and the filling is bubbling. (In case the edges of the piecrust begin to brown too soon, cover them with aluminum foil to keep them from burning.) Let completely cool before cutting so that the slices are firm.

NOTAS

✱ *You can use store-bought pie dough, although the piecrust in this recipe has a different flavor and texture because it includes eggs.*

✱ *The amount of sugar needed in the filling will depend on how sweet the pineapple is. If your pineapple is pretty sweet, add only ½ cup (100 g) of sugar.*

ROLLO DE FRESA

Strawberry Cream Roll

This roll cake is a beloved dessert in the cities along the Gulf of Mexico and a staple at local bakeries in places such as Tampico and the Port of Veracruz. This version, with strawberries, is the classic and most popular one, followed by the mango and peach variations. There is also one that is stuffed with a medley of fruits. In my hometown of Tampico, we know it as *rollo de fresa* (strawberry roll), but it is also known as *brazo de reina* (queen's arm) and *niño envuelto* (wrapped baby).

PREP TIME: 25 minutes plus 4 hours and 30 minutes resting and chilling time	**COOK TIME:** 15 minutes	**YIELD:** 8 servings

½ cup (1 stick/115 g) unsalted butter, melted and cooled, plus more for greasing

¾ cup (150 g) granulated sugar

2 teaspoons vanilla extract, divided

6 large eggs, whites and yolks separated

½ cup (65 g) all-purpose flour, sifted

3 teaspoons baking powder

2½ cups (600 ml) cold heavy cream

1/3 cup (40 g) confectioners' sugar (or more if you like it sweeter)

1 pound (454 g) strawberries (see Notas), trimmed and cut into small pieces, leaving some whole or sliced for decoration

NOTAS

- *This cake can also be filled with strawberry jam instead of chopped strawberries.*
- *Refrigerating the cake before serving allows you to cut perfect slices of cake.*

1. Preheat the oven to 400°F (205°C). Place a large metal bowl in the refrigerator or freezer to chill. Line an 11 x 16-inch (28 x 41 cm) rimmed baking sheet with buttered parchment paper. (I like to be generous with the butter to avoid any accidents with the batter.)

2. In a medium bowl, combine the granulated sugar, 1 teaspoon of the vanilla, and the egg yolks and beat until the mixture changes to a light-yellow color. In a separate medium bowl, combine the flour and baking powder and mix well. In a large bowl, beat the egg whites until they form firm peaks. Use a wire whisk to slowly integrate the egg yolk mixture into the egg whites. Next, use a rubber spatula to fold in the flour. Finally, fold in the melted butter. Pour the batter into the prepared baking sheet, evenly smoothing out the batter so that it touches all sides.

3. Bake for 12 to 15 minutes, until the cake begins to shrink and separate from the sides of the pan and has a light-golden color. Remove from the oven and cover the cake with a moistened kitchen towel. Immediately and carefully invert the baking sheet over a flat surface (so that the towel is under the cake). Remove the pan and parchment paper. Slowly and tightly roll the sponge cake from one short end to the other without pressing it. Let cool completely while rolled and wrapped in the towel.

4. While the cake is cooling, beat the heavy cream in the chilled bowl with an electric mixer until it begins to form firm peaks. Add the confectioners' sugar and the remaining 1 teaspoon vanilla and continue to beat until the cream is stiff. Cover the bowl and refrigerate until ready to assemble the cake.

5. Unroll the cooled cake and spread an even layer of whipped cream on top, reserving whipped cream to decorate the outside. Place the chopped strawberries all over the whipped cream. Carefully roll the cake up tightly with the help of the towel, leaving the cake seam side down.

6. To decorate the cake, first place it on a serving plate because once it is decorated, it will not be easy to move to another plate. Using a spatula, spread the remaining whipped cream over the top and sides of the roll and garnish with the whole or sliced strawberries. Refrigerate for at least 4 hours before serving (see Notas).

MEXICAN WEDDING COOKIES

These cookies are not common everywhere in Mexico, but they are occasionally given as party favors to wedding guests in the northern states of Mexico. They are also made during the holidays and make an excellent treat to pack in cellophane bags to gift to friends and relatives.

PREP TIME: 25 minutes	**COOK TIME:** 18 minutes	**YIELD:** 36 cookies

1 cup (2 sticks/225 g) unsalted butter, softened, plus more for greasing

2 cups (240 g) pecan halves (see Notas)

2 cups (260 g) all-purpose flour

½ teaspoon salt

⅓ cup (40 g) plus 1½ cups (190 g) confectioners' sugar, divided

1 teaspoon vanilla extract

FOR SERVING
Milk

NOTAS

* *You can use walnuts instead of pecans.*

* *The dough can be made a day in advance and refrigerated. When ready to bake, bring the dough to room temperature before forming the cookies and baking them.*

* *Many recipes instruct to roll the cookies in the confectioners' sugar while they are still warm. I've found that if you coat the cookies in the sugar when they are cool, they look prettier and don't get a gummy texture.*

1. Preheat the oven to 325°F (165°C) and grease two large baking sheets with butter (or line with parchment paper).

2. Place the pecans in a food processor or blender and chop finely. Remove 1 cup (120 g) of the chopped pecans and process the rest into a very fine texture, almost like cornmeal. (Be careful not to overprocess the pecans or you will end up with pecan butter.)

3. In a large bowl, combine the flour, salt, and all the pecans and combine well.

4. Using a hand mixer, in a separate large bowl, beat the butter with ⅓ cup (40 g) of the confectioners' sugar until light and fluffy, then stir in the vanilla. Gradually add the flour-pecan mixture and beat on low speed for a few seconds, or until it forms a coarse dough that resembles oatmeal (see Notas). (Do not overwork the dough, as it will result in a flat cookie.)

5. Roll 1 tablespoon of dough into a small ball, about 1 inch (2.5 cm) in diameter. Repeat to form the rest of the cookies and place them about 1½ inches (4 cm) apart on the prepared baking sheets.

6. Bake for 15 to 18 minutes, until the bottoms begin to brown and the cookies are firm. Let cool for 3 minutes on the baking sheets, then transfer to a wire rack to cool completely.

7. Place the remaining 1½ cups (190 g) confectioners' sugar in a bowl. Place 2 or 3 cookies in the bowl and roll them in the sugar to coat, shaking off any excess sugar if necessary. Roll again to completely coat them (see Notas). Store in an airtight container at room temperature for up to 2 weeks.

8. Serve with milk.

CAPIROTADA

Capirotada is a special holiday dish that is often described as a bread pudding. It is popular before and during Lent, as well as the winter holidays, and you can find many variations of it throughout Mexico. Capirotada is usually made in a round baking dish and formed by layering slices of toasted bread and a variety of toppings, such as nuts, crumbled cheese, and raisins. It is then soaked in a syrup made with piloncillo, cloves, and cinnamon before being baked. Capirotada is one of the many recipes brought to the New World by the Spaniards. A dish with a heavy Moorish influence, it was originally prepared as a way to use leftover bread.

PREP TIME: 20 minutes	**COOK TIME:** 50 minutes	**YIELD:** 10 servings

12 ounces (340 g) piloncillo (about 1¼ cups if shredded) or 1½ cups (340 g) dark brown sugar

1 stick Mexican cinnamon

2 whole cloves

3 tablespoons salted butter, melted

3 tablespoons vegetable oil

16 slices (⅓ inch/8.5 mm thick) Bolillo (page 215), French, Italian, or challah bread, at least 2 days old

¾ cup (90 g) crumbled queso Cotija (see Notas)

¼ cup (40 g) salted roasted peanuts (see Notas)

¼ cup (35 g) raisins (see Notas)

2 bananas, sliced (optional)

¼ cup (48 g) rainbow sprinkles (optional)

2 tablespoons butter, cut into small cubes

1. Preheat the oven to 350ºF (175ºC). Make the syrup by placing the piloncillo, cinnamon stick, cloves, and 1½ cups (360 ml) of water in a medium saucepan over medium-low heat. Stir occasionally and let the piloncillo melt into a light syrup, about 20 minutes. Once melted, remove the saucepan from the heat and let cool, then strain the syrup through a fine-mesh strainer.

2. While the syrup is cooking, in a small bowl, combine the melted butter with the oil, mix well, and brush the mixture over both sides of the bread slices. Place the bread slices on a baking tray and bake for 8 minutes, then flip them over to bake for 5 more minutes, or until a deep-golden color (see Notas). Remove from the oven and keep the oven on.

3. In an 8-inch (20 cm) round oven-safe dish, make a single, flat layer of bread. Using a ladle, slowly pour syrup over the bread, making sure that all the bread pieces absorb the syrup and reserving enough syrup for the second layer of bread. Alternatively, dip each slice of bread into the syrup to ensure that the crumb is evenly soaked in the syrup. Top this layer of bread with half of the cheese, peanuts, raisins, and sliced bananas (if using). Make a second layer of bread and pour the remaining syrup over it. Top with the remaining cheese, peanuts, raisins, and banana slices (if using). Add the sprinkles (if using).

4. Dot the capirotada with the cubes of butter, then cover the dish with aluminum foil and bake for 40 minutes, or until the top crust is golden and the lower layers are still moist. Serve warm or cold (see Notas).

NOTAS

✖ *In northern Mexico, some people use toasted corn tortillas instead of bread. Traditionally, the bread is fried instead of toasted in the oven, but I find that toasting the bread is faster and less messy.*

✖ *You can substitute the Cotija cheese with Mexican Manchego, Chihuahua, Monterey Jack, mild white Cheddar, and even Parmesan mixed with queso fresco.*

✖ *Instead of peanuts, you can use almonds, pecans, walnuts, or pine nuts. Prunes, cranberries, or other dried fruit can be used instead of raisins. You can also add shredded coconut.*

✖ *Some cooks also add anise seed to the syrup. To try this, use ¼ teaspoon.*

✖ *Some other common fruits for topping are Plátanos Fritos (page 174) and apples. If you want, you can top the capirotada with even more toppings at serving time.*

TORREJAS

Torrejas consist of thick slices of bread that are dipped in milk and a fluffy egg mixture and fried. The result is a slightly crispy exterior and a moist, soft interior. They are then dunked in a sweet piloncillo syrup, making for a delectable dessert. The recipe originally came from Spain and was adapted in Mexico with the addition of the piloncillo syrup. It is popular during Christmas and Easter and can also be enjoyed for breakfast or brunch as a "Mexican French toast."

PREP TIME: 15 minutes	**COOK TIME:** 25 minutes	**YIELD:** 10 torrejas

PILONCILLO SYRUP

12 ounces (340 g) piloncillo (about 1¼ cups if shredded) or 1½ cups (340 g) dark brown sugar

1 stick Mexican cinnamon

TORREJAS

10 thick slices (⅔ inch/2 cm thick) Bolillo (page 215) or Italian bread, preferably day-old (see Notas)

3 large eggs, separated whites and yolks

Pinch of salt

2 cups (480 ml) vegetable oil

1½ cups (360 ml) whole milk

1. To make the piloncillo syrup: Place the piloncillo, cinnamon stick, and 1 cup (240 ml) of water in a medium saucepan over medium-low heat and let the piloncillo melt, stirring occasionally, into a light syrup, about 20 minutes (see Notas). Remove the pan from the heat and discard the cinnamon stick.

2. Meanwhile, make the torrejas: Heat a comal over medium-high heat. Lightly toast the bread slices until they have a light-golden color. This will help them keep their shape as they soak up the wet ingredients.

3. Place the egg whites in a large bowl and add the salt. Using an electric mixer, beat the egg whites for 4 to 5 minutes, until they start forming peaks. Continue beating the egg whites while slowly adding in the egg yolks, one at a time, until they are well incorporated with the egg whites, 1 to 2 minutes.

4. In a medium or large skillet, heat the oil over medium-high heat. Pour the milk into a medium bowl, then very quickly dip 1 slice of bread into the milk, making sure that the bread does not absorb too much milk. Next, using kitchen tongs, dip the slice into the egg mixture to completely coat it. Place the bread in the hot skillet and cook for about 30 seconds, then flip to cook the other side—it should be a medium light-golden color. Transfer to a paper towel–lined plate to absorb any excess oil. Repeat this step with the remaining bread slices. (If you are using a large skillet, you can cook several slices at the same time.)

5. Once all the bread slices are cooked, quickly dip them into the piloncillo syrup, place them on plates, and pour a little more of the syrup over each torreja. Serve hot, warm, or at room temperature.

NOTAS

✳ *Use a bread that has a dense crumb texture so that it will hold its shape during the cooking process and at serving time. Day-old bread is recommended because it is drier and thus holds its shape when soaking up the ingredients. Slice the bread the night before and leave it on your counter covered with a cloth napkin to dry out.*

✳ *When making the syrup, be sure the heat does not go above medium (medium-low is preferred). If the heat is too high, the syrup will boil and reduce too much.*

✳ *For a more aromatic and flavorful syrup, add 2 whole cloves, a pinch of anise seeds, and 1 star anise. You can also add orange peel or zest, or allspice berries.*

✳ *Some people make torrejas without the syrup and only dust them with sugar or cinnamon sugar. Others like to add vanilla extract and even orange peel to the milk.*

GORDITAS DULCES

Gorditas dulces are a sweet comforting treat that are more commonly found in people's homes than in restaurants. They're a warm, cookie-like dessert that were often made by my mom, and as a result, they bring back the memories of childhood whenever I make them. *Gorditas dulces* means "sweet gorditas," but they don't have much in common with savory gorditas. Because they more closely resemble a cookie, I like to call them "griddle cookies" in English. These gorditas dulces are more common in the northern regions of Mexico, where they are thin and crispy (in other parts of the country, they are thicker and fluffier).

PREP TIME: 10 minutes plus 30 minutes resting	**COOK TIME:** 20 minutes	**YIELD:** 20 gorditas

½ stick Mexican cinnamon

2 cups (260 g) all-purpose flour

½ cup (100 g) sugar

¾ cup (155 g) shortening

NOTAS

✱ *Not everyone makes these sweet gorditas with cinnamon tea—this is the way my mom made them. You can use plain warm water instead of the tea.*

✱ *The dough keeps well in an airtight container in the refrigerator for about 2 days, or it can be frozen for up to 1 month.*

1. Place the cinnamon stick and 1 cup (240 ml) of water in a small saucepan and bring to a boil over medium-high heat to make cinnamon tea (see Notas). Once it starts boiling, reduce the heat to low and let simmer until the water starts changing to a very light caramel color, 6 to 8 minutes. Remove from the heat and discard the cinnamon stick. Let cool to room temperature.

2. In a large bowl, combine the flour and sugar and mix well. Add the shortening in small pieces. Using your hands, combine the shortening with the flour-sugar mix until the mixture resembles coarse crumbs. Slowly add 6 tablespoons of the cooled cinnamon tea over the mixture, a little at a time, and knead the dough until it sticks together. If the dough does not come together, stir in a little bit more of the cinnamon tea, 1 teaspoon at time, until the dough comes together and has a nice, smooth texture.

3. Wrap the dough in plastic wrap and refrigerate for at least 30 minutes to help develop the gluten and make it easier to form them into circles. When ready to make the gorditas, let the dough sit on the counter for about 10 minutes.

4. Heat a comal or large griddle over medium-high heat. Divide the dough into 20 small balls, each about the size of a golf ball. Keep the balls of dough covered with a plastic wrap. Place a dough ball between two 7 x 7-inch (18 x 18 cm) sheets of plastic cut from a freezer bag. Using a tortilla press (or a heavy glass pie dish), press down on the ball. Remove the top piece of plastic and lift the cookie up using the bottom piece of plastic. Flip the plastic over and place the gordita over the palm of your other hand. Remove the plastic sheet.

5. Carefully place the gordita onto the hot comal and cook for at least 1 minute on each side and up to 1½ to 2 minutes depending on its thickness. (Be careful while flipping the gorditas, as they are very fragile. Use a thin spatula to do this.) Carefully remove it from the comal and place on a plate or in a basket lined with a cloth kitchen napkin. Repeat this process with the remaining dough balls.

6. Let the gorditas cool and turn crispy before eating. You can store the cookies in a plastic bag in the refrigerator for up to 1 week.

MANTECADAS

Mexican Muffins

Mantecadas are a type of muffin that are a staple in the world of Mexican sweet breads and can always be found in bakeries alongside Conchas (page 206) and other sweet breads. They are commonly enjoyed in households during the afternoon coffee time, but they are also great for breakfast. I like to make them plain, but you can also top them with chopped pecans or add raisins to the batter. This recipe is quick and easy to make for when I'm craving a sweet bread for my afternoon coffee or have last-minute guests stopping by. They are also a great gift to bring to friends when I don't want to show up empty-handed! Once you discover the versatility of the humble mantecada, you'll see why many continue to make this recipe again and again.

PREP TIME: 10 minutes plus 15 minutes resting time	**COOK TIME:** 20 minutes	**YIELD:** 6 mantecadas

1 cup minus 1 tablespoon (122 g) all-purpose flour

1 teaspoon baking powder

1 teaspoon instant yeast

2 large eggs

½ cup plus 1 tablespoon (125 g) sugar

½ cup (120 ml) whole milk

1 teaspoon vanilla extract or orange essence (see Nota)

1 teaspoon orange zest (optional)

½ cup (120 ml) vegetable oil

Pinch of salt

NOTA *Every baker chooses a flavoring of their choice when making mantecadas—it could be vanilla, orange, cinnamon, or almond. My favorite flavoring is orange essence.*

1. Preheat the oven to 400°F (205°C). Line a 6-cup muffin pan with paper liners.

2. In a medium bowl, mix the flour, baking powder, and yeast until well combined.

3. In a large bowl, whisk together the eggs and sugar until the sugar has dissolved. Add the milk, flavoring of your choice, and orange zest (if using) and whisk to combine. Incorporate the oil in a gentle stream, whisking to form a homogenous mixture.

4. Slowly stir the dry ingredients into the wet ingredients along with the pinch of salt, mixing gently until a uniform batter forms. (Do not overmix.) Let the batter rest for 15 minutes.

5. With the help of a pitcher or a ladle, pour about ½ cup (120 ml) of the batter into each of the prepared muffin cups, filling them to just a little bit below the top edge.

6. Bake for 20 minutes. Remove from the oven and let cool for about 5 minutes on a cooling rack.

7. Serve warm or at room temperature. Store for 2 to 3 days in an airtight container.

CONCHAS

Among all the different kinds of traditional *pan dulce* (sweet bread) that you can find in Mexican bakeries, *conchas* are without a doubt the most popular, recognizable, and representative of Mexico and its love of bread. For years, I have practiced this recipe to get the right texture. The name *concha* means "shell" because of its sweet topping that resembles the surface of a seashell.

PREP TIME: 25 minutes plus 1 hour and 45 minutes resting time	**BAKING TIME:** 20 minutes	**YIELD:** 16 conchas

DOUGH

3¾ cups (488 g) all-purpose flour (see Notas on page 208), plus more to prevent sticking and for dusting

2½ teaspoons (7.5 g) active dry or instant yeast (see Notas on page 208)

½ cup plus 2 tablespoons (125 g) granulated sugar

½ teaspoon salt

2 large eggs

1 teaspoon vanilla extract

½ cup (120 ml) warm milk (see Notas on page 208)

½ cup (1 stick/115 g) unsalted butter, at room temperature, plus more for greasing

Shortening, for greasing

TOPPING

½ cup plus 1 teaspoon (100 g) shortening

⅞ cup (100 g) confectioners' sugar

1 cup (130 g) all-purpose flour

1 teaspoon ground cinnamon (optional)

1 teaspoon unsweetened cocoa powder (optional)

1. To make the dough (read the Notas on page 208 before you begin): Measure out all the dough ingredients. In the bowl of a stand mixer, combine the 3¾ cups (488 g) flour, yeast, granulated sugar, and salt. Turn the mixer on medium speed, just enough to mix the ingredients well. Add the egg and vanilla extract, then gradually add the warm milk, a little at a time, while continuing to mix until the dough reaches a cohesive consistency. Add the butter and continue beating on medium speed for about 7 minutes, to ensure all the ingredients are well incorporated and the dough will be smooth. To prevent the dough from sticking, sprinkle 2 or 3 tablespoons of additional flour around the inside of the bowl to help it separate from the bowl easily. The desired texture of the dough is soft and slightly sticky. (Avoid adding too much flour, as it can make the dough too stiff.)

2. Transfer the dough to a lightly floured work surface, then knead it just enough to shape it into a ball. Place the ball in a large bowl greased with butter. Cover it with plastic wrap or wax paper and a cloth kitchen napkin. Let the dough rest in a warm place for about 1 hour, or until it doubles in size. (Be patient and do not proceed to the next step until the dough has doubled in size.)

3. Meanwhile, make the topping: In a medium bowl, soften the shortening with a spatula until it is very creamy, then add the confectioners' sugar and mix well. Stir in the 1 cup (120 g) flour, a little at a time, along with the cinnamon (if using), until it is well incorporated and has a paste-like consistency. (If you are making half of the conchas with chocolate topping, then divide this paste in half and add the cocoa powder to one half, mixing until it well incorporated.)

(continued)

4. Once the dough has doubled in size, place it onto a lightly floured work surface and let rest for about 5 minutes. Divide the dough into 16 equal-size pieces, about ¼ cup (60 g) of dough each. To shape into balls, lightly flour your hands, then place a dough piece on the work surface and gently press down on it with your hand, rotating your hand to form the ball. Place onto a baking sheet greased with shortening (you will need two greased baking sheets). Repeat this step with the remaining dough pieces. Using your hands, grease the top of each ball with a little shortening. (Do not skip this step, as it will help the sugar topping adhere to the dough.)

5. To add the topping, lightly flour your hands and divide the topping paste into 16 equal-size pieces and form into balls. Use your hands to press down on each ball to form a small, flat circle (I like to use a sheet of plastic from a freezer bag, like when making tortillas). Place this disc onto a ball of dough and press down very firmly. Repeat with the remaining balls of paste. Use a concha cutter or a knife to decorate the topping with the traditional concha pattern. Let the conchas rest in a warm place until they have almost doubled in size, 45 minutes to 1 hour. (Do not let them rise any longer or they will collapse when baking. Meanwhile, preheat the oven to 325ºF (165ºC).

6. Bake for 20 minutes, or until the bottoms are lightly golden. (If placing more than one baking sheet in the oven at a time, rotate them after 10 to 12 minutes; move the sheet on the bottom rack to the top rack and vice versa to achieve even baking.) Let the conchas cool for a few minutes to allow the topping to set.

7. Serve at room temperature.

NOTAS

* *While imperial units are provided, I recommend using the weight measurements in parentheses for accuracy.*

* *Consider using bread flour for a softer and fluffier texture in your bread. Adjust the milk quantity based on the type of flour used, as different flours absorb liquid differently.*

* *When using active dry yeast, first proof it in ½ cup (120 ml) lukewarm milk for 10 to 15 minutes.*

* *If you want to make all the conchas with a chocolate topping, use 2 teaspoons of cocoa powder. You can also add food coloring for colored toppings.*

* *Resting the dough is critical for achieving good results with this recipe. The second rest time will be shorter than the first. If your kitchen is cold, the dough will take longer to rise.*

* *If you don't want to make all the conchas at the same time, you can divide the dough and freeze a portion of it for later by storing it in a freezer bag for up to 2 weeks. Defrost it overnight before shaping the conchas. Alternatively, you can freeze shaped conchas with the topping on them (while still uncooked). Place them on a tray to freeze, then once frozen, store them in a freezer bag. Defrost them until they rise, then bake according to the recipe.*

ROSCA DE REYES

Three Kings Bread

Every January 6, Día de los Reyes (Epiphany) is celebrated in Mexico, when we enjoy this special bread, usually accompanied by *chocolate caliente* (Mexican hot chocolate). Inside the bread is a small plastic doll representing the baby Jesus, and the person who finds the doll in their slice is designated to cook tamales on February 2, Día de la Candelaria (Candlemas). This tradition, although rooted in religion, is widespread and cherished throughout the country regardless of anyone's background. Mexican bakeries are bustling during this time of the year, selling delicious roscas for people to enjoy at home, work, and school. For many Mexicans living outside of Mexico, making this bread at home helps us feel closer to our loved ones during this important season. The texture of "modern" roscas found in Mexican bakeries today is light and airy compared to the texture of roscas of old. This recipe is for a more old-fashioned version.

PREP TIME: 25 minutes plus 2 hours and 15 minutes resting time	**COOK TIME:** 25 minutes	**YIELD:** 16 servings

STARTER

½ cup (120 ml) lukewarm water

1 packet (2¼ teaspoons/7 g) active dry yeast

½ cup (60 g) bread flour

DOUGH

3½ cups (440 g) bread flour, plus more if needed and for dusting

¾ cup (150 g) granulated sugar

¼ teaspoon salt

3 large whole eggs

2 egg yolks

1½ tablespoons orange extract or orange blossom water

Zest of 1 orange

¾ cup (170 g) unsalted butter, softened, plus more for greasing

2 or 3 plastic baby dolls (optional; see Notas)

Shortening, for greasing

1 large egg, beaten, for glazing

1. To make the starter: Pour the lukewarm water into a medium bowl and sprinkle in the yeast. Stir until the yeast has dissolved, then let stand until foamy, 5 to 10 minutes. Stir in the ½ cup (60 g) bread flour and cover the bowl with plastic wrap. Let rest in a warm place until doubled in volume, about 25 minutes.

2. To make the dough: In a large bowl or the bowl of a stand mixer, mix the 3½ cups (440 g) bread flour, the ¾ cup (150 g) granulated sugar, and the salt. Add the whole eggs, egg yolks, orange extract, and orange zest and mix until well incorporated. If using a stand mixer, mix with the dough hook attachment on low (speed 2). If not using a stand mixer, mix the dough by hand on a work surface.

3. Add the starter and mix with the dough. Add the butter and continue mixing until the dough is soft and sticky but still manageable. Add more flour if needed. On a lightly floured work surface, knead the dough until it is smooth, very soft, and slightly wet. (Avoid adding too much flour, as it can make the bread dry.) Place the dough in a separate large bowl greased with butter and cover with buttered plastic wrap. Let rest in a warm place until doubled in size, about 1½ hours (or longer, if needed).

(continued)

TOPPINGS

7½ tablespoons margarine or shortening

½ cup plus 3 tablespoons (100 g) confectioners' sugar

1 cup (130 g) all-purpose flour

Assorted dried fruits (such as figs, candied citron, quince paste strips, and green and red candied cherries; see Notas)

¼ cup (50 g) granulated sugar

FOR SERVING

Mexican hot chocolate

4. Meanwhile, prepare the toppings: For the sugar paste decoration, in a medium bowl, use a spatula to mix the margarine with the confectioners' sugar until creamy. Slowly add the all-purpose flour while continuing to mix until a smooth paste forms.

5. Once the dough has doubled in size, turn the dough onto a lightly floured work surface. First shape into a round cushion-like ball, then make a hole in the middle using your hands and spread it out to form a large ring. Insert the plastic dolls (if using) so that they are enclosed in the dough, and transfer the ring to a large baking sheet greased with shortening. Loosely cover the bread with buttered plastic wrap and let rise in a warm place for 45 minutes, or until almost doubled in volume.

6. Preheat the oven to 325°F (165° C) for at least 20 minutes before baking. Set the baking rack in the middle of the oven.

7. Once the bread has almost doubled in size, brush the top with the beaten egg, then allow it to dry and apply a second coat. (The egg not only helps the decorations stay in place as the dough rises, but it also adds a beautiful golden hue to the crust.)

8. Form strips out of the sugar paste and place them on the bread to decorate it. Add the dried fruit and press them gently onto the surface of the dough. Sprinkle the ¼ cup (50 g) granulated sugar on top of the bread.

9. Bake for 25 to 30 minutes, until the crust is golden brown. (Depending on your oven, it may require more time.) Let cool completely before slicing.

10. Serve with Mexican hot chocolate.

NOTAS

✖ *Ensure that your kitchen is warm to help the dough rise. If the dough doesn't double in volume after the specified time, allow it to rest longer until it reaches the desired size.*

✖ *Bakers usually add 2 or 3 baby dolls to a rosca this size. You can also insert the plastic baby dolls into the bottom of the bread after it has been baked (and it has cooled). You can find the baby dolls at hobby/craft stores, usually in the baby shower section. If you can't find them, substitute them with pecans, walnuts halves, or dried fava beans.*

✖ *If you can't find traditional decorations, you can use prunes, pecans, walnuts, or fruit cake mix.*

TAMALES DE ELOTE
Sweet Corn Tamales

These delicious tamales are a seasonal dessert in Mexico and are usually made during the fall corn harvest, when the freshest and sweetest corn is available. Many people eat these tamales in the morning for breakfast or during the evening coffee time (often called *merienda*). I like to top them with sour cream and crumbled queso fresco, but you can also top them with a drizzle of condensed milk, or even salsa and cheese for a savory treat.

PREP TIME: 30 minutes	**COOK TIME:** 1 hour and 15 minutes	**YIELD:** 16 tamales

6 large ears corn (see Notas), with husks on

1½ cups (150 g) masa harina for tortillas (see Notas on page 214)

1¼ cups (2½ sticks/280 g) unsalted butter, at room temperature

½ cup (100 g) sugar

1 teaspoon baking powder

1 teaspoon salt

FOR GARNISHING (OPTIONAL)

Sour cream or Mexican crema

Crumbled queso fresco (or Cotija)

1. Carefully remove the husks from the corn, making sure not to tear them, because you will be using them to wrap the tamales. Place the husks in a large pot, cover them with hot water, and let soak to soften and make pliable, about 20 minutes. (You can place a heavy plate on top of the husks to keep them submerged inside the pot.)

2. While the husks soak, remove the kernels from the corncobs, then place them in a blender or food processor and coarsely grind them so that they are medium-coarse (see Notas).

3. Place the masa harina in a large bowl along with the ground corn kernels.

4. In a separate bowl, use an electric mixer (or mix by hand with a spatula) to beat the butter and sugar until the mixture is fluffy and creamy. Add the butter mixture to the bowl with the masa harina. Add the baking powder and salt and mix well until the dough is well combined and has the texture of fluffy mashed potatoes.

5. Remove the husks from the pot and pat them dry with a kitchen towel. Select the large ones to use for wrapping the tamales, and the small ones to line the steamer (see Notas).

6. To assemble the tamales, spread about ¼ cup (60 g) of dough onto the center of a corn husk. Fold the sides of the corn husk inward and then fold the narrow end up toward the center of the tamal. Place the formed tamal on a tray while you assemble the remaining 15 tamales.

(continued)

7. To steam the tamales, place a steamer rack inside a large stockpot. Add enough warm water up to the level of the steamer rack, then line the rack with a layer of corn husks. Place the tamales in the pot in an upright position, with the open ends facing up. Cover them with a generous layer of the remaining husks, then cover the pot with the lid. Steam the tamales for 1 hour and 15 minutes over medium-high heat. During the steaming, check the pot to see if it has enough water (be careful when removing the lid), adding more if needed (see Notas). To check if the tamales are ready, remove one from the pot using kitchen tongs and let sit on a plate for 5 minutes. (This will give the dough a chance to solidify after coming out of the steaming pot.) After the waiting time, open the tamal. If the husk separates easily from the dough, that means the tamal is ready; if the dough sticks to the husk, place it back in the pot and cook for 15 more minutes.

8. Serve while they are still hot and top with sour cream and crumbled cheese, if desired.

NOTAS

- *The corn found in Mexico has a much higher starch content than the corn found in the United States, which is why masa harina is added to the dough when using corn outside of Mexico. I recommend allowing the fresh corn to dry out in the refrigerator for a day or two after buying it. This way you won't need to use as much masa harina to form a cohesive dough.*
- *The 6 large ears of corn should render about 6 cups (870 g) of corn kernels, which is the amount needed to make this recipe. Some corn is very juicy and can acquire a soupy consistency after being processed in the blender. If this is the case, add some more masa harina to the dough.*
- *If the corn husk you're using to assemble a tamal is too small, overlap two of them. If you don't have enough fresh corn husks, you can use dried corn husks instead.*
- *If you need to add more water to the pot when steaming the tamales, make sure to pour it as close to the side of the pot as possible, avoiding the tamales. If water gets into the tamales, they will lose their flavor and the dough will be soggy.*
- *You can store the tamales in plastic bags in your freezer for up to 4 months. To reheat, allow the tamales to defrost, then place them in a steamer for 10 to 15 minutes. You can also pop them in the microwave on the high setting for about 1 minute.*

BOLILLOS

A lot of countries have a versatile crusty bread in their cuisine, and Mexico is no exception. The humble *bolillo* is found everywhere and plays many roles in our gastronomy. It can be served on the table to accompany stews and other dishes, as well as used to make tortas. It is also a main ingredient in recipes such as Molletes (page 40) and Capirotada (page 198). Bolillos are medium-size rolls with an oblong shape and tapered ends. They are soft on the inside and crusty on the outside. Their crumb is good at absorbing liquids, such as soups, sauces, stews, hot chocolate, and champurrado. In my hometown of Tampico, it is common for people to cut open a bolillo and butter the halves before toasting them, making for a scrumptious complement to their morning coffee, especially on Sunday mornings. Baking bolillos requires the same attention to detail that all leavened breads demand. It took a while for me to develop a recipe that replicates the bolillos from Mexican bakeries, but the effort was worth it in the end.

PREP TIME: 30 minutes plus 11 hours and 40 minutes resting time	**COOK TIME:** 20 minutes	**YIELD:** 10 bolillos

STARTER

½ teaspoon instant or active dry yeast (see Notas on page 216)

1 cup (125 g) bread flour (see Notas on page 216)

DOUGH

3 cups (375 g) bread flour (see Notas on page 216), plus more for dusting

1½ teaspoons instant or active dry yeast (see Notas on page 216)

2 teaspoons salt

¼ cup (50 g) shortening (see Notas on page 216), melted and cooled, plus more for greasing

1 cup (240 ml) warm water

Vegetable oil, for greasing (optional)

4 cups (1 quart/950 ml) warm water, plus more for spraying

FOR SERVING

Butter

1. To make the starter: The night before baking, combine the ½ teaspoon yeast with ¾ cup (180 ml) of water in a small bowl, then add the 1 cup (125 g) flour and mix thoroughly. Cover the bowl with plastic wrap and let it sit on the kitchen countertop overnight, or for at least 8 hours. (This starter will enhance the flavor of the bread.) The following morning, the starter should have increased in volume and developed lots of bubbles.

2. To make the dough: In a large bowl or the bowl of a stand mixer, combine the starter, the 3 cups (375 g) flour, the 1½ teaspoons yeast, the salt, and the melted shortening and mix well. Begin kneading the dough, gradually adding the warm water at the start of the kneading process. If using a stand mixer, knead for 7 to 8 minutes with a dough hook attachment on low (speed 2). The dough will start to come together and pull away from the sides of the bowl as you knead it. It should be cohesive but still slightly sticky. Remove the dough from the bowl and place it on a work surface. If hand kneading, work the dough on a lightly floured work surface for approximately 15 minutes. Shape the dough into a ball. It should feel soft but have a slightly rough texture.

(continued)

3. Grease a separate large bowl with shortening or oil, then place the dough inside, rotating it to ensure that all sides are coated with the grease. Cover the bowl with plastic wrap and let rest in a warm place for about 2 hours, or until the dough has doubled in size. (In warm and humid climates, this process may take less time.) Once the dough has doubled in size, gently deflate it by pushing your fist into it. Divide the dough into 10 equal-size pieces (each weighing about 110 grams) and place on a work surface slightly greased with shortening. Cover the pieces with plastic wrap greased with shortening and let rest for 15 minutes. (Resting them will help the gluten develop and make it easier to shape the bolillos.)

4. To shape the bolillos, lightly dust the work surface with flour. Take 1 piece of dough and flatten it using the palm of your hand, then fold one-third of the dough toward you and press it down firmly with your fingers to seal it well. Repeat this folding and sealing process until you have formed a roll, making sure to pinch the dough tightly to seal all the ends securely. To shape the tips, gently but firmly place your hands over the dough, cupping your fingers, and roll it back and forth. As you do this, press the heel of your hands to leave some dough uncovered, forming the traditional bolillo ears. Place seam side down on a greased baking sheet and cover with greased plastic wrap. Repeat for the remaining dough pieces, then let rise until they have almost doubled in size, about 45 minutes.

5. Meanwhile, place a metal tray on the oven floor and fill it with the warm water. Preheat the oven to 450° F (230°C). (The water in the pan should be creating steam by the time you put the bolillos in the oven.) Once the bolillos have almost doubled in size, and right before placing them in the oven, make a deep, long lengthwise cut in each one with a sharp serrated knife or a razor blade. Place 2 inches (5 cm) apart on large baking sheets and spray with warm water. Bake for 20 minutes, or until golden brown. Let cool on a wire rack.

6. Serve warm or at room temperature with butter. The bread will stay fresh for a couple of days if stored in a plastic bag or airtight container. Alternatively, you can freeze it for up to 1 month (see Notas).

NOTAS

✳ *If using active dry yeast, dissolve it first with ¾ cup (180 ml) of water, mix well, and let it proof for 5 minutes.*

✳ *If you don't have bread flour, you can use all-purpose flour. The crumb will be denser, but the bolillos will still be great.*

✳ *Traditional bolillo recipes don't include shortening or any other sort of fat; however, adding shortening helps preserve the softness of the bread for more days.*

✳ *To reheat the bread after freezing it, lightly thaw it, then spray it with room-temperature water. Reheat at 400°F (205°C) oven until crispy again, 12 to 15 minutes.*

✳ *This recipe yields 10 bolillos, but feel free to double it if you want to make a larger batch.*

DRINKS

CUCUMBER LIME AGUA FRESCA

Agua fresca literally translates to "fresh water," and this agua fresca takes freshness to the next level. The combination of cucumber and lime makes this one of the most refreshing beverages you can prepare, and the perfect drink for hot summer days. Plus, it looks beautiful when garnished with mint and a fresh slice of cucumber and is ideal for picnics, parties, barbecues, and any summer gathering.

PREP TIME: 10 minutes plus 1 hour chilling time	**YIELD:** 16 servings

1 large English cucumber or 2 common cucumbers (see Notas), peeled

½ cup (120 ml) fresh lime juice (4 to 6 limes, depending on their size and juiciness)

⅔ cup (135 g) sugar

3 cups (420 g) ice cubes

FOR GARNISHING

Lime and/or cucumber slices

3 small sprigs fresh mint (optional; see Notas)

1. Using a spoon, remove the seeds from the cucumber(s). Chop the cucumbers into chunks and place them into a blender along with the lime juice, sugar, and 3 cups (720 ml) of water. Process for a couple of minutes until a smooth mixture.

2. Pour the mixture through a fine-mesh strainer into a large pitcher, pressing down on the strainer with the back of a spoon to extract as much liquid as possible. Discard the residue in the strainer.

3. Add 3 more cups (720 ml) of water along with the ice cubes to the pitcher, stir, and refrigerate for 1 hour.

4. Pour the agua fresca into glasses, add some lime and/or cucumber slices to the glasses or on the rims, and garnish with a few mint leaves (if using).

NOTAS

✱ *Use any type of cucumber available to you, just make sure to remove the seeds or strain the liquid after processing it in the blender.*

✱ *I like to garnish this agua fresca with mint sprigs, but some people add mint to the blender in step 1.*

AGUA DE MANGO

Mango Agua Fresca

Agua de mango is one of the countless varieties of *aguas frescas* that you can find throughout Mexico. The type of fruit used for fruit-flavored aguas frescas can vary depending on the region or the season. This mango agua fresca perfectly highlights the soft and sweet flavor of this magnificent fruit, so I highly recommend you try it when mangoes are in season.

PREP TIME: 10 minutes	**YIELD:** 10 cups (2.4 L)

2 cups (330 g) peeled and chopped ripe mango of choice (about 4 medium mangoes) (see Notas)

½ cup (100 g) sugar, plus more if needed (see Notas)

3 cups (320 g) ice cubes

1. Add the chopped mango to a blender along with the sugar and 5 cups (1.2 L) of water. Process until smooth.

2. Pour the mixture into a large pitcher and add the ice cubes. Taste the drink to check for sweetness and add more sugar if needed.

3. Serve immediately or refrigerate the pitcher for 30 minutes if you want to serve it very cold.

NOTAS

* ✶ You can use any type of mango for this recipe.

* ✶ Different varieties of mangos will have different levels of sweetness, so adjust the sugar accordingly.

SPARKLING LIMEADE AND ORANGEADE

Besides sodas and aguas frescas, another popular type of drink in Mexico is limeade, along with orangeade. Both of those drinks are available at many restaurants throughout Mexico. We refer to these drinks as *limonada preparada* (prepared limeade) and *naranjada preparada* (prepared orangeade). The "prepared" term comes from the fact that these drinks are usually prepared from scratch when ordered and made using freshly squeezed fruit as opposed to powdered mixes.

PREP TIME: 10 minutes	**COOK TIME:** 5 minutes	**YIELD:** 1 serving

SIMPLE SYRUP (SEE NOTA)

1 cup (200 g) sugar

LIMEADE OR ORANGEADE

½ cup (70 g) ice cubes

2 tablespoons fresh lime juice or ½ cup (120 ml) fresh orange juice

1 cup (240 ml) cold mineral water or club soda

1. To make the simple syrup: Place the sugar and 1 cup (240 ml) of water in a small saucepan over medium-high heat and bring to a boil, stirring until the sugar dissolves. Once boiling, after about 3 minutes, reduce the heat and let simmer for 5 minutes, or until it turns into a uniform syrup. Remove from the heat and let cool, about 5 minutes. Store in an airtight container in the refrigerator.

2. To make the limeade or orangeade: Place the ice cubes in a tall glass, pour in the juice (either lime or orange), and add 2 tablespoons of the cooled simple syrup.

3. Slowly pour in the mineral water, or it will form bubbles and rise to the top.

4. Stir well and serve.

NOTA *I prefer to use simple syrup because it dissolves faster in the mineral water, but these drinks are commonly made at home using granulated sugar. I recommend using 1 tablespoon of granulated sugar for 2 tablespoons of simple syrup. You can also use store-bought simple syrup.*

LICUADO DE NOPAL CON PIÑA

Cactus and Pineapple Juice

This green cactus juice has been around for decades in Mexico, where it holds a special place in the country's culture. This juice, and others like it, is commonly sold at local *refresquerias*, juice and smoothie shops that are open during the early hours of the day. If you visit one of these juice stands and order a *licuado de nopal*, you will be asked what fruits you would like to add, with pineapple and orange being the most common choices. One of the reasons behind the popularity of this beverage is the many health benefits that *nopales* have been found to have. Besides containing fiber, vitamins, and antioxidants, nopales are known to have digestive benefits, anti-inflammatory properties, and the ability to help aid in regulating blood sugar.

PREP TIME: 10 minutes	**YIELD:** 1 serving

1 medium fresh (raw) nopal, cleaned and chopped into small pieces (see page 11 for nopales prep)

1 slice pineapple (about ¾ inch/ 2 cm thick), cut into cubes

1 cup (240 ml) fresh orange juice

1 sprig fresh parsley

¾ cup (105 g) ice cubes

1. Place the nopal, pineapple, orange juice, and parsley in a blender and process until a fine texture.

2. Add the ice cubes to a large glass and pour in the juice, using a fine-mesh strainer if the drink has too much pulp (see Notas).

3. Store any leftover juice in the refrigerator to enjoy the next day. (Some people like to make enough to store in a pitcher in the fridge for up to 3 days.)

NOTAS

* *If using a high-powered blender, you may not need to use a fine-mesh strainer when pouring the juice. If you are fine with pulp and want to get that extra fiber, there's no need to strain the juice.*

* *If fresh pineapple is not available, you can use frozen pineapple chunks.*

* *You can add your favorite fruits and/or vegetables to this juice, such as apple, pear, kale, cucumber, celery, and spinach. You can also add a little fresh lime juice.*

ATOLE DE TAMARINDO

Tamarind Atole

Atoles are masa-based drinks that are served hot, usually in the morning or at night. Besides the regular white atole, there are myriad flavored atoles that can be found throughout Mexico. They often incorporate local fruits or nuts to create the different flavors. Tamarind trees are found in the tropical areas of Mexico, such as in the states of Jalisco and Colima, which are big producers of this fruit. However, tamarind atole can be found almost anywhere that atole is sold, as it is one of the most common flavors. I believe that it's probably the combination of the sweet-and-sour flavors that make it so popular. On top of being one of the most popular, this drink is also my favorite atole.

PREP TIME: 5 minutes plus 30 minutes soaking time	**COOK TIME:** 15 minutes	**YIELD:** 4 servings

4 ounces (113 g) tamarind pods, without the shells

1¼ cups (300 ml) warm water

½ cup (100 g) sugar

½ cup (50 g) masa harina (see Nota)

1. Soak the peeled tamarind pods in a medium bowl with the warm water for 30 minutes. After that time, rub the tamarind pods between your fingers to separate the pulp from the seeds. Leave the pulp in the bowl to mix with the water.

2. Pour 4 cups (1 quart/950 ml) of water into a medium saucepan and add the sugar. Add the tamarind mixture, passing it through a fine-mesh strainer to remove the seeds. Place the saucepan over medium heat and bring to a boil.

3. Meanwhile, place the masa harina in a small bowl with ¾ cup (180 ml) of water. Stir well to dissolve any lumps.

4. Once the tamarind mixture is boiling, gently add the masa harina mixture, stir, and let come to a boil again, then reduce the heat to low and simmer while stirring frequently for about 8 minutes, until the atole is thick. (The atole consistency is similar to a thick gravy; if it becomes too thick, add more water to thin it out.)

5. Serve in mugs. Be careful before drinking, as its thick consistency keeps the drink very hot for a long time.

NOTA *Use the masa harina sold for making tortillas.*

ATOLE DE NARANJA
Orange Atole

Some people may be pleasantly surprised to discover what a delightful drink this orange atole is. This *atole de naranja* is commonly found in the northern part of the state of Veracruz, a region with abundant citrus production, and a cup is perfect for warming you up on a cold winter morning, all while giving you some extra vitamin C.

PREP TIME: 10 minutes	**COOK TIME:** 20 minutes	**YIELD:** 4 servings

6 tablespoons masa harina for tortillas (see Notas)

2 cups (480 ml) fresh orange juice (see Notas)

4 tablespoons sugar (see Notas)

1. Place the masa harina in a small bowl and add 1 cup (240 ml) of water. Stir well to dissolve any lumps.

2. In a medium saucepan, combine the orange juice, 1 cup (240 ml) of water, and the sugar and bring to a boil over medium-high heat. Once boiling, reduce the heat to a gentle simmer, then once it starts simmering, stir in the masa harina mixture, making sure everything is well combined. Cook over medium-high heat, stirring frequently, until it starts to thicken, then reduce the heat to low and continue simmering for 5 more minutes.

3. Serve in mugs. Be careful before drinking, as its thick consistency keeps the drink very hot for a long time.

NOTAS

✖ *The brand or type of masa harina that you use will affect the thickness of the final drink.*

✖ *If you are using store-bought orange juice, use less sugar than indicated. Store-bought juice is usually sweeter than fresh-squeezed oranges.*

✖ *You can substitute the sugar with ⅓ cone of piloncillo (about 75 g).*

✖ *For additional flavoring, add ½ stick of cinnamon or some ground cinnamon to each mug at serving time.*

TEPACHE

Tepache is a fermented drink made with pineapple peels, water, piloncillo, and cinnamon sticks. It is very tasty and, when served with a lot of ice cubes, an effective way of tackling the summer heat waves. The golden-brown color, refreshing mouthfeel, and slight alcoholic content (as a result of the fermentation; 2 to 4 percent ABV) frequently make people compare this drink to beer. During the 2020 pandemic, some jurisdictions in Mexico imposed a temporary ban on the sale of alcoholic drinks, and as a result, "homemade tepache" became a popular recipe almost overnight. The key is letting the ingredients ferment for the right amount of time; the process takes about two days, although where you live and the climate you have will affect that, so you must keep an eye on it. Read all the Notas for more indications on the fermenting process.

PREP TIME: 10 minutes plus 36 to 48 hours fermenting time	**YIELD:** 8 cups (2 quarts/1.9 L)

Peel of 1 pineapple

1 piloncillo cone, cut into pieces (or 1 cup/220 g light brown sugar)

1 stick Mexican cinnamon

3 whole cloves

Ice

NOTAS

* If you live somewhere hot without air conditioning, check the tepache after 12 hours instead of 24. The fermentation time given in this recipe takes into account an average room temperature of 77 to 86°F (25 to 30°C). A warmer environment will accelerate the fermentation process and a cooler one will slow it down to 3 to 4 days.

* If you feel that the taste is too strong, dilute the tepache with equal parts water.

* The quantities in this recipe can be multiplied to make a larger amount.

1. In a large glass pitcher or container, place the pineapple peel, piloncillo, cinnamon stick, cloves, and 8 cups (2 quarts/1.9 L) of water.

2. Cover the pitcher with cheesecloth or plastic wrap in a loose manner so that the brew can breathe. Place on your countertop and let sit for 24 hours (see Notas). After this time, check it and, with a wooden spoon, remove the white foam that has formed on top of the liquid. Loosely cover it again and let rest for another 24 to 36 hours. DO NOT let it ferment any longer; otherwise it will turn into pineapple vinegar.

3. Strain the liquid with a fine-mesh strainer from the pitcher into another pitcher that is filled with lots of ice. Taste for sweetness and add sugar if desired. If not drinking the tepache right away, store it in the glass pitcher, covered, in your refrigerator to enjoy later. Just do not wait too long to drink it, because it will keep fermenting in the refrigerator.

4. Serve in glass mugs with lots of ice.

FROZEN MANGO MARGARITA

Besides the classic *margarita*, nowadays you can find many great frozen margarita cocktails made with an array of fruits, including watermelon, pineapple, strawberry, and, of course, mango. This frozen mango margarita is a fun and flavorful drink to make for parties, gatherings, or just a casual Friday night at home with friends. It's incredibly easy to make, and the best part is that you can make it any time of the year because it uses frozen mango.

PREP TIME: 10 minutes	**YIELD:** 4 servings

16 ounces (454 g) frozen mango chunks (see Notas)

6 ounces (180 ml) tequila blanco

3 ounces (90 ml) triple sec

8 tablespoons sugar (see Notas)

2½ ounces (75 ml) fresh lime juice

4 cups (560 g) ice cubes

FOR GARNISHING (OPTIONAL)

½ teaspoon coarse salt

½ teaspoon chile piquín powder or cayenne pepper

1. Place the mango, tequila, triple sec, sugar, and lime juice in a blender and process on the highest setting until a smooth mixture. Add the ice cubes to the blender, making sure they reach the bottom where the blades are, and continue blending until the mixture is very smooth.

2. Pour the frozen margarita into four glasses and serve. If using, mix the salt and chile piquín powder and sprinkle some of the mixture on top of each margarita.

NOTAS

* If you come across fresh, ripe mangos, peel the fruit, chop it into pieces (removing the pit), and place it in the freezer for a minimum of 4 hours. Then proceed with the instructions In the recipe.

* Sometimes frozen mango isn't very sweet, so adjust the amount of sugar accordingly.

TEQUILA SUNRISE

Although this colorful beverage was invented in California, it certainly knows how to embrace the Mexican spirit with its use of tequila. It also happens to be my absolute favorite cocktail recipe, and one that I've prepared countless times for guests. A tequila sunrise is a sweet and refreshing cocktail made with orange juice, grenadine, and tequila. I love that it's incredibly easy to make and uses ingredients that are easily found in most kitchens.

PREP TIME: 5 minutes	**YIELD:** 1 serving

1 cup (140 g) ice cubes

2 ounces (60 ml) tequila blanco

5 ounces (150 ml) fresh orange juice (see Notas)

¾ ounce (45 ml) red grenadine (see Notas)

FOR GARNISHING

1 Maraschino cherry

1 orange wedge

1. Fill a tall glass with ice (you can use a highball glass). Pour in the tequila and orange juice and stir.

2. To get the "sunrise" color effect, slowly pour the grenadine into the glass without stirring (this step needs to be slow!).

3. Garnish the glass with the cherry and orange wedge. Cheers!

NOTAS

✳ *A good substitute for the orange juice is pineapple juice.*

✳ *If you can't find red grenadine, you can use pomegranate juice concentrate, or mix cranberry juice with simple syrup (see step 1 on page 223 for the recipe or use store-bought). Keep in mind that the "sunrise" color effect may not look as good if you're not using grenadine.*

✳ *For a nonalcoholic version, skip the tequila and add 2 ounces (60 ml) of mineral water.*

ROASTING VEGETABLES

Roasted vegetables add a depth of flavor to salsas and sauces. Here's a quick guide to roasting vegetables for the recipes in this book.

ANCHO/GUAJILLO PEPPERS: Clean the peppers with a damp kitchen cloth. Cut a slit along the length of the peppers using a knife or kitchen scissors, then remove the seeds and veins. Place the peppers open wide on a hot comal or skillet over medium-high heat and slightly roast them for 30 to 40 seconds. If needed, use a spatula to press them down. The peppers will release their aroma when they are ready. Remove promptly.

ÁRBOL PEPPERS: Place the peppers on a hot comal or skillet over medium-high heat and turn them 2 to 3 times until they start releasing their aroma and their skins change to a lighter color, 20 to 30 seconds. Remove promptly.

GARLIC CLOVES: Keeping the peel on, place the cloves on a hot comal or skillet over medium-high heat for about 1 minute, turning them two or three times to roast evenly. The peel will be charred. Remove promptly. Peel the garlic before use.

ONIONS: Place the onion slices or quarters on a hot comal or skillet over medium-high heat for about 1 minute, turning them once. They will look charred and the texture will be slightly softened. Remove promptly.

POBLANO PEPPERS: Place the peppers over an open flame on your stove over medium-high heat for 5 to 6 minutes, turning them with kitchen tongs to roast evenly. The peppers will have charred skin all over and look slightly soft. After roasting, place the peppers in a plastic bag and close it to steam them for 5 minutes. This process makes the skins of the peppers loosen up for easy removal.

Remove the peppers from the bag and scrape off the charred skins by rubbing your fingers on the surface of the pepper or using the edge of a spoon. You can leave some of the charred skins on, if you like, to add more flavor to the dish. Do not rinse the peppers, as they will lose some of their flavor. With a sharp knife, cut a slit along the length of the peppers, then remove the seeds and veins. Alternatively, you can place them on a hot comal or skillet over medium-high heat for 8 to 10 minutes, turning them to roast evenly, or place them on a baking sheet under your broiler at 400°F (205°C) for 2 minutes, turning them once. An outdoor gas or charcoal grill can also be used. After roasting, continue with the steaming process.

SERRANO/JALAPEÑO PEPPERS: Place the peppers on a hot comal or skillet over medium-high heat for 5 minutes for serrano peppers and 7 to 8 minutes for jalapeños, turning them every 2 minutes or so to roast evenly. Their skins will have a semisoft texture.

TOMATILLOS: Place the tomatillos on a hot comal or skillet over medium-high heat for 6 minutes, turning them every 2 minutes or so to evenly roast. They will have a very soft texture.

TOMATOES: Place the tomatoes on a hot comal or skillet over medium-high heat for 8 minutes, turning them every 2 minutes or so to roast evenly. They will look charred all over and have a semisoft texture. They should be semi-cooked. For a large tomato that still looks raw after roasting, wrap it in a piece of aluminum foil for about 5 minutes to finish cooking in its steam.

RECIPE REFERENCE

Here's a list of the recipes found in my first book, *The Mexican Home Kitchen*. I mention a lot of these recipes throughout this book, so I thought it would be helpful to include them here as a starting point, especially if you're looking for a particular recipe.

TORTILLAS
Corn Tortillas
Flour Tortillas

RICE & BEANS
Arroz Blanco (White Rice)
Arroz Rojo (Red Rice)
Arroz Verde (Green Rice)
Frijoles de Olla (Beans From the Pot)
Frijoles Pintos Cremosos (Creamy Pinto Beans)
Frijoles Refritos (Refried Beans)

SALSAS
Pico de Gallo
Salsa Roja (Red Salsa)
Salsa Roja Rostizada (Roasted Red Salsa)
Salsa Taquera (Taqueria-Style Salsa)
Salsa Verde (Green Salsa)
Salsa Verde Cremosa (Creamy Avocado Tomatillo Salsa)
Salsa Verde Rostizada (Roasted Green Salsa)

SOUPS
Caldo de Pollo (Chicken Soup)
Caldo de Res (Beef and Vegetable Soup)
Crema de Elote (Cream of Corn Soup)
Crema de Papa (Cream of Potato Soup)
Menudo (Mexican Tripe Soup)
Pozole Rojo (Red Pozole)
Pozole Verde de Pollo (Green Pozole with Chicken)
Sopa de Fideo (Mexican Noodle Soup)
Sopa de Lentejas (Lentil Soup)
Sopa de Tortilla (Tortilla Soup)

MAIN DISHES
Beef
Albondigas (Mexican Meatball Soup)
Albondigas en Chipotle (Meatballs In Chipotle Sauce)
Barbacoa de Lengua (Beef Tongue Barbacoa Tacos)
Bistec a la Mexicana (Mexican-Style Steak)
Carne con Papas (Beef and Potatoes)
Empanadas de Carne Molida (Ground Beef Empanadas)
Milanesa de Res (Beef Milanesa)
Picadillo
Ropa Vieja (Shredded Beef In Tomato Sauce)
Tacos de Bistec (Steak Tacos)

Chicken
Enchiladas Verdes (Green Enchiladas)
Ensalada de Pollo (Chicken Salad)
Mole Poblano
Pollo a la Veracruzana (Chicken Veracruz-Style)
Pollo en Salsa Verde Con Calabacitas (Chicken with Squash in Green Salsa)
Pollo Entomatado (Chicken in Tomato Sauce)
Tamales de Pollo en Salsa Verde (Chicken in Green Salsa Tamales)
Tinga de Pollo (Chicken Tinga)
Tostadas de Pollo (Chicken Tostadas)

Pork
Asado de Puerco (Pork Stew)
Calabacitas con Puerco (Pork Stew with Squash)
Carnitas
Chicharrón en Salsa Verde (Fried Pork Skins in Green Salsa)
Costillas en Salsa Verde (Pork Rib Tips in Green Salsa)

Ensalada de Coditos (Macaroni Salad)

Frijol con Puerco (Pork and Beans)

Tamales de Puerco (Pork Tamales)

Tamales de Rajas con Queso (Cheese and Vegetable Tamales)

Mixed Meats

Discada Norteña (Northern-Style Mixed Meats)

Seafood

Camarones en Chipotle (Shrimp In Chipotle Sauce)

Filete de Pescado Empanizado (Breaded Fish Fillet)

Vegetarian

Chiles Rellenos

Empanadas de Queso (Cheese Empanadas)

Enchiladas Rojas (Red Enchiladas)

Entomatadas

Flautas de Papa (Crispy Rolled Potato Tacos)

SIDES

Calabacitas con Crema (Mexican Squash with Cream)

Calabacitas con Queso (Mexican Squash with Cheese)

Ensalada de Repollo (Cabbage Salad)

Guacamole

Nopales con Oregano (Cactus Paddles with Oregano)

DESSERTS

Arroz con Leche (Rice Pudding)

Budín de Pan (Bread Pudding)

Buñuelos

Churros

Crepas (Crepes)

Flan

Gelatina de Mosaico (Mosaic Gelatin)

Pastel de Cumpleaños (Old-Fashioned Birthday Cake)

Pastel de Tres Leches (Three Milks Cake)

Tamales de Piña (Pineapple Tamales)

Tamales Dulces (Sweet Tamales)

DRINKS

Agua de Horchata (Horchata)

Agua de Jamaica (Hibiscus Iced Tea)

Agua de Tamarindo (Tamarind Drink)

Atole Blanco (White Atole)

Atole de Arroz (Rice Atole)

Café de Olla (Mexican Spiced Coffee)

Champurrado

Chocolate Caliente (Mexican Hot Chocolate)

Ponche Navideño (Mexican Christmas Punch)

INDEX

ACKNOWLEDGMENTS

I am incredibly thankful and humbled to have been able to write this second book, which would not have been possible without the overwhelming response to my first book, *The Mexican Home Kitchen*, as well as the continued support of my readers. Thank you to everyone who enjoyed and shared the recipes in my first book, and asked me for the second one. This is for you.

To my dear mother and grandmother, thank you for teaching me what would become the foundation of my knowledge of this great cuisine.

To the wonderful people that I have met throughout Mexico who have been kind enough to share their recipes, tips, and techniques with me, thank you for sharing your wisdom.

My deepest appreciation to Erin Canning and the entire team at The Quarto Group. Thank you for always being patient with me, and for continuing to support my passion of sharing the Mexican gastronomy with the world.

Thank you to my husband for always being a big supporter of all my endeavors, and to my sister Adriana, who contributed some of the photos in this book.

Last, but certainly not least, I owe a special thanks to my dear son, David. Without his invaluable contributions and support, most of this book would not have been possible. We worked together as a team, and I am immensely proud of what we have achieved together. Thank you for being an integral part of this project.

Thank you all for your love and support, and keep passing these recipes down to the next generations.

ABOUT THE AUTHOR

A former school teacher, **MELY MARTÍNEZ** was born and raised in the coastal city of Tampico, Tamaulipas. She has been interested in food since a very young age, and her experience in the kitchen was formed while helping her mother cook at home for their large family, as well as during summer visits to her grandmother's farm in Veracruz. As an adult, further travels throughout Mexico helped Mely broaden her knowledge of Mexican cuisine and deepen her interest in the country's gastronomy.

In 2008, Mely started her blog, Mexico in My Kitchen, where she shares traditional Mexican recipes so that they can be passed down and preserved for new generations, as well as shared with all food lovers. Based on the continued success of her blog, Mely was inspired to write her first cookbook, The Mexican Home Kitchen, which was released in 2020.

Throughout the years, Mely's passion for Mexican cuisine has led her to curate a vast collection of vintage Mexican cookbooks dating as far back as the nineteenth century. She has also participated in several courses, workshops, and seminars on Mexican gastronomy and its history from prestigious institutions, such as the Escuela de Gastronomía Mexicana and the INAH (Instituto Nacional de Antropología e Historia) in Mexico as well as the CIA (Culinary Institute of America) in the United States.

Besides writing for her blog, Mely also teaches Mexican cooking classes online and serves as a consultant to chefs and restaurateurs around the world.

She divides her time between her home in Dallas and her frequent travels throughout Mexico.